TURNING SURVIVAL INTO WORDS

FROM HOUSES OF FEAR TO FREEDOM

Boni Woodland

Turning Survival Into Words
From Houses of Fear to Freedom
Copyright © 2026 Boni Woodland
All rights reserved.

For privacy reasons, names and locations have been changed.

Printed in the United States of America

Published by: Boni Woodland
Design & layout: Mariah Miller Creative Services

ISBN: 979-8-218-90659-7

PenAndBrushInk

penandbrushink@gmail.com
www.painterandthreads.com

Table of Contents

ACKNOWLEDGMENTS

I am grateful to every person who helped me move forward, in big and small ways, on my long walk toward a better life. If I have forgotten anyone, it is my memory that failed, not my gratitude.

With love to Scot Woodland, my children, all who have called me Mom, and my grandchildren—present in my heart, no matter the distance. Danny Fossan, for the car you loaned us. Karen Pignata, for always being there. Kim Woodland, Kathie Beckham, Pat Sibley, Buffy Nickolson, Cynthia Smith, Joanne Hild, Nory Fussell, Trishele Swasey, for the hope and kindness offered. Gail Samcoff, who never once forgot my birthday. Mary Tyler, who has since passed, and David Dobrinen for kindness in high school.

Thank you, Bruce Kirk, an instructor at Yuba College, and his auto shop students, who kept my old car alive; the tow-truck drivers who came to my rescue more times than I can count, and the local food banks that helped feed us at times. A special thank you to my therapist for bump-starting my healing journey.

My deep thanks to my editors: JL Buddy, Mila Johansen, Rhonda Douglas, Simona Casele, and Mariah Miller for guiding this story into its final shape.

And to Ender, who waited so patiently for me to finish this book before we could go outside and play ball again.

Disclaimer

This book reflects the author's lived experiences, memories, and personal interpretations. While care has been taken to provide accurate citations and references, the author makes no representation or warranty that all details are complete or free from error. This content also represents only my lived experience, and not all of the issues found in domestic violence experiences.

The content is offered for informational and educational purposes and is not intended as legal, medical, or professional advice. Any interpretations of historical or legal matters are based on publicly available sources cited within the book. The author expressly disclaims liability for any loss, damage, or disruption caused by reliance on this work. Readers are encouraged to consult appropriate professionals for guidance on personal, legal, or health matters.

Content Warning

This book contains discussions of domestic abuse, sexual violence, and emotional trauma. Although I share these experiences to illuminate, inspire hope, and aid others, some readers might find certain passages upsetting. Please take care while reading and know that support resources are available if needed.

A Note for Readers

I use the term "The Husband" as a placeholder rather than a name, and I also use numbers for my sons rather than their names. This choice is both practical and protective. My intent is not to expose or injure anyone with what I write, but to tell my story as truthfully as I can. By leaving out certain names, I can share the realities I lived without causing unnecessary harm to those I still care for, even when our paths have been painful or complicated.

I've framed my story through the houses I lived in, each one holding its own chapter of struggle, change, and survival. The walls and rooms became landmarks of my journey, showing the different aspects of abuse and how I moved through fear towards freedom.

Human memory is fragile; it reshapes itself over time. I acknowledge that some details may not be entirely accurate. However, I also carried a diary through much of this journey, and those pages remind me of what really happened. This book rests in the space between recollection and record, between what I lived and what I wrote down at the time.

This book is written as a story, but you'll also find notes and resources gathered at the back. Citation numbers will point you to further information on the footnote pages. The footnotes provide legal context and background for readers seeking a deeper understanding of the systems and laws that have shaped my experiences. The notes and resources are here to give clarity and connection, while the story itself conveys the heart of what I lived through.

INTRODUCTION

The night I left, the house stood silent and empty behind me. It wasn't just a *house* I walked away from. It was a life, a lie, a weight I couldn't carry for one more day. I didn't have a real plan.

Didn't have a hope, really. Just a quiet voice inside me that said, "Anything is better than this."

Some say houses are just wood, plaster, and nails, but I know better.

Houses remember. They remember the footsteps of those who walked their floors and the sounds of the voices that once filled their rooms. They hold stories in their walls. They echo back your prayers, your cries, your silence, *and your laughter, if you are lucky.*

Some houses are warm with love. Others, well, others learn how to keep secrets.

Every house I lived in taught me something: how to shrink, disappear, or smile while surviving. But this book isn't just about surviving. It's about the slow becoming of a woman who finally realized she could choose something different. About the breaking of locks and beliefs.

For me, home was never a place of safety; it represented a place of control, fear, and survival.

I learned that sometimes, *leaving* is the only way to live.

In one, I finally heard that quiet voice whispering, *"GO."* This book is about the moment I listened and what it cost to be free.

"Owning our story and loving ourselves through that process is the bravest thing that we'll ever do."

~ Brené Brown

PROLOGUE

Don't Breathe, Don't Blink

I lay curled on the old sofa, still as stone. My eyes closed, my breath shallow, pretending.

I hadn't heard the sound of his bare feet, but I felt a shift in the air, the prickly feeling of being watched, and from the barest slit under my lashes, I saw him. I peeked at his silhouette towering over the sofa, quietly watching me. I didn't dare move or speak. I lived with his words echoing in my mind. *"If I could have found you, I would have killed you,"* he had stated, flicking away his cigarette.

It was one of the many times fear had frozen me. The living room where he had now relegated me to sleep was dark, but the moonlight touched him with silver. It showed me his still looming form and glittering eyes. I felt his deep hatred and my confusion over it. I couldn't understand why he didn't move or say something. What did he want? Minutes passed, maybe more, but time stretches like elastic when you're trying not to breathe.

I had planned to leave soon to escape with my sons. A tiny flicker of hope was buried beneath layers of exhaustion, fear, and the numb routine of our lives. I had made it through the drinking years, the apologies, the rage, the stonewalling, gaslighting, and the silence. I had survived. But freedom, it turns out, is not just a door you walk through; *you have to know you can.*

My church forbade divorce, and my childhood home had long since closed its doors to me. To be one of God's chosen, you had to live your life according to his plan, and leaving your husband is not part of the plan.

Friends? Who could have friends in such a life as the one we had carved out? The quiet of the night surrounded us, and still, he stood staring. My body felt his deep emotion. Cold sweat trickled between my breasts. I wanted to run, run crazily out the door and down the road into that silver moonlit night. But my sons lay sleeping in the next room, and there was no way I was leaving them.

The planned escape had initially been for them. But now it was for me, too, and everything that had kept me both moored and captured in this crazy life was about to be tossed away. Freedom, I had found out, was something I deserved, my sons deserved, and it was worth fighting for.

That night, relegated to the sofa, I knew there would be no reconciliation. His request for a marital separation was a ploy, another tool to force compliance with his demands. But they were magic words to my ears. If he didn't want me anymore, *then by our church doctrine, I was free!*

I didn't know then how far I'd have to go to reclaim my life. I only knew that whatever courage I had left had to rise up now, quietly, carefully, shifting from a breeze into a storm of fierce action and awakening.

This is the story of how not to live and what it cost me to believe I didn't deserve more.

Chapter One

The First Click

The ushers in the church clicked the locks on the large meeting room doors. The Minister announced that, for our safety, the doors would now remain closed and locked during services. Unfortunately, some non-believers had gotten the idea that we were participating in extreme religious rituals, possibly animal sacrifice ... who knew? The thought made me laugh inside.

Instead of anything sinister, we sat every Saturday for two hours with Bibles and notebooks in our laps, furiously writing down notes from the sermons we listened to. Children played on blankets at their parents' feet as we learned how to live a life pleasing to God, the farthest thing from animal sacrifice I could imagine. But the rumors were persistent.

In some of our worldwide churches, nonbelievers had tried to force their way in and disrupt meetings. This generated enough concern to warrant locking the doors.

Non-believers had labeled us a cult.[1]

The room instantly went silent when we all noticed the ushers standing guard by the doors. Even the babies seemed to sense something and quieted. To console us, the Minister opened the dictionary and read aloud the definition of a cult. He insisted we did not fit the label because we believed in Jesus Christ. His conclusion was simple: some people were just small-minded, and as we'd been taught, Satan was always prowling about, trying to take us down.

At the time, I felt a strange sense of comfort, believing that being sealed in meant we were protected. But now, when I think of those locked doors, I see them as the first click of a much larger lock that would come to surround my life.

Just a couple of years in the future, the world would be shocked by the tragedy of Jonestown, when Jim Jones led nearly his entire congregation to die under the weight of manipulation, despair, and a poisoned drink, which some were forced to consume.[2] *That*, everyone agreed, was a *cult*. Our church clucked its collective tongue, pointing a knowing finger. *Not like us. That was a real cult.* Even as we nodded in agreement, something inside me whispered otherwise. We didn't drink their particular beverage but we had swallowed our own flavor of control and fear.

There were no fences or armed guards but there was plenty of spiritual gatekeeping. If Jonestown was the Major Leagues of mind control, we were the Minors. Less fatal, perhaps, but still dangerous in quieter, more acceptable ways.

Looking back, I realize that not everything we were taught was straight from Scripture. Some rules may have had roots in the Bible. Others grew from the *eisegesis*,* interpretations of our ministers, and still more ideas seemed to sprout from each family's private soil, their personal fears, need for control, or misguided devotion. The church handed out the seeds, but every household grew its own version of the garden, some with more weeds and thorns than others. We were a large, self-described family with all the dysfunction that befalls families in wider society: rivalry, infighting, backstabbing, and gossip—the elixir drink of the congregation!

Like many other churches, ours started with a man who heard God's call to start this new church because the world needed it. Ours was a unique blend: part Judaism, part Christianity (but not enough to be considered mainstream of either,) plus a hefty dose of British Israelism, fundamentalism, and authoritarianism.

By the time I was old enough to understand church, God, and our beliefs, I felt lucky. Our family had been called to be among the chosen because my dad had heard the church leader on the radio. Apparently, it was as simple as that. You could listen to a man's voice on the radio call you to a specific church, and if you showed up, you were chosen. There were thousands of us all around the world, waiting for the fulfillment of prophecy and the return of God.

The overarching rule against forming close friendships with "worldly people" meant we invested all our time in the church. There were potlucks after services, dances, weddings, get-togethers at each other's homes, and holidays, all spent together. It was as if we were a world within the world, with clearly defined rules and roles for living.

The older I got, the more my mind whispered: *What do you mean we can't dance with the black brethren? We eat with them. We sit in services with them.* Many other insidious thoughts found their way into my questioning mind. Suspicion grew.

How could the church declare we were all one if we had to be segregated? And why did the church leaders wear makeup on their television shows when we were not allowed to wear it at all? There were more inconsistencies, but even dwelling on those thoughts felt risky. I didn't want to be labeled a heretic. My world was already lonely enough. I couldn't imagine being kicked out of the church. It was all I knew.

Since childhood, I had wanted to remain a member in good standing, with all my heart.

So, hearing those church doors lock made me feel safe and wanted, on the inside. I didn't know it then, but this was the first lock; there would be others.

Eisegesis: Reading your own ideas into the Bible instead of drawing meaning out of the text and the culture at the time the words were written.

Chapter Two

The Proposal

No Satan Necessary. We Got This.

By the time I was old enough to leave home, I had no road map. The Church had taught me what purity meant, but not what love was. I had never been kissed, never been courted. At twenty-one, I was still waiting for someone to notice me.

Back then, we were supposed to wait, to save ourselves for marriage. Purity was supposed to guarantee holy love and a fantastic sex life untouched by the sin of fornication. Who didn't want that?

Our pastor said the end was near. Prophecies were being fulfilled; God could return any day. We were promised new, spiritual bodies in the world to come. No hunger. No pain. But alas, no sex. What hung over us like a storm cloud wasn't only the fear of no sex itself, it was the constant warning that time was running out, that we might miss the things everyone else said we were supposed to want.

As hungry teenagers, this felt like staring at an amazing banquet of "food through a window" we would never get to eat from. Nearly every service reminded us that this world was going to end. Maybe even tomorrow.

What I feared was the possibility of never getting to experience all the things everyone else made such a big deal about. Maybe in some subtle way, that fear nudged some of us to get married before we were ready. Which is precisely what we did.

So, later on, when a boy from the church finally noticed me and reached out to me in his car, one hand on the stick shift, the other gripping the steering wheel, with an important, life-changing question on his lips, something in me tilted. Even though part of me hesitated and felt like a passenger in my own life, I leaned towards what I thought was love.

I didn't know that this moment, his sudden proposal of marriage for our future, would lead us down a painful road that would rival anything Satan could have dreamed up. But the truth was, we didn't need Satan's help. We were perfectly capable of building our own hell.

He had picked me up unexpectedly that day and seemed to be brewing with some heavy conversation that left a knot in my belly and sweat on my palms. His angst was shimmering in the air. I thought maybe I had done something wrong; perhaps he meant to tell me he wanted to break up. In the back of my mind, it might have been a little relief, although to be rejected yet again in life would have been painful.

Finally, he spoke. He asked me to marry him. His eyes were fixed straight ahead. His hand still rested on the stick shift. There was no ring, no buildup, just a flat question that landed in my lap like a stone. I felt confused, even let down. This wasn't how I imagined such a serious question would be asked. Shouldn't there be more fanfare? More romance? Why was he jumping to marriage now?

My mind spun. I wasn't seeking marriage. I had barely begun to live. But someone had finally, finally noticed me. That felt like a miracle. The thrill of being wanted filled a hollow place inside me that had always ached. I didn't have the life experience to imagine a future with anyone; I barely knew who I was.

For the first time, being with this boyfriend, I felt something like normalcy, a small sense of belonging I had never known inside my own family. My family and our cult-like religion had always warned us to stay apart from the world; the world is not godly! That belief had made a very lonely life. However, I wasn't worried. My boyfriend attended our church, followed the same rules, and shared the same beliefs. We would not be unequally yoked.

Our church always told us we were God's chosen ones, set apart from the rest of the world. The message was simple: stay obedient, stay separate, and life would go better for us. For someone as lonely as I was, belonging anywhere, even by following strict rules, felt like something I couldn't afford to lose. So, when someone finally noticed me, it felt too precious to risk losing.

In that moment, when he asked me to marry him, and I didn't answer right away, the silence between us thickened. I felt myself freeze, unsure of what to say, unsure of what I was even allowed to feel.

At that time, I didn't know I was selling myself cheap. I had never been offered more, or taught that love should be tender, mutual, or respectful. We were both reaching for the same low bar, blind to the higher ones that could have changed everything.

A part of me sensed something was off, a small flicker of disappointment I couldn't quite name. I didn't have the language for what I was feeling, only a quiet, uneasy sense that something wasn't right.

Then he cut through the silence with a cold, flat sentence: *"Well, if you don't want to marry me, I'll just go find someone else."*

The silence that followed closed around us. His words stung. His expectation hung in the air between us, pressing on me harder than the question itself.

In my immaturity and lack of worldly knowledge, I eventually said yes. That's what my life had taught me so far: saying no to someone always led to something worse.

What I Did Not Know

We were still practically kids, pretending we knew what adulthood even looked like. Two sheltered souls caught in a rush of something that felt new and exciting. I had never learned negotiation, never participated in conversations that discussed compromise. I had actually never seen that come into play in my family life. If I'm honest, we hadn't discussed anything in a mature, emotional way. We were busy feeling and experiencing something new.

My parents' relationship had soured me on the whole idea of marriage. It was a farce held together by duty and resentment. Their mutual disdain for each other gave me a bitter taste for the very concept. They each used me as their personal confidant against the other, sharing things better said to a therapist and not my confused ears. In my young mind, I thought they had chosen commitment over genuine love.

If I had a free-thinking mind that could have envisioned a future beyond marriage and children, or a friend who could see what I couldn't, maybe I would have escaped that car before my life took its turn. Perhaps someone would have said, "You don't have to do this. You both have other choices."

I like to think I would have listened. Perhaps not right away, but those words might have stayed with me, whispering louder than my own fear. But I had no one like that. No friend that felt safe to confide in, no voice that spoke in faith instead of rules. I didn't know that you could say no and still be loved.

What I needed was faith in myself and someone who could talk with me without commandments or criticism. However, my life had never provided me with those tools, or the means to build them myself.

We both felt the tension building, and I think he expected me to be more excited. I sat in the passenger seat of the car, feeling myself shrink. The situation had gotten out of control, and I didn't have the words to express my heart.

I secretly speculated that I could undo it later if I said yes now. My heart yearned for a boyfriend and craved these moments with him, away from my home, that he offered. It was an incredibly new experience for me. With him, I didn't feel so terribly alone.

The power of having someone say they love you is mesmerizing.

This boyfriend took me away from a house full of contradictions. From a family that kept church rules on Saturdays and broke them the rest of the week. He took me away from the abuse. The danger. The strife.

I had no idea what love was supposed to feel like, only that this was the closest thing I'd ever felt.

But the truth?

I did not know what I did not know.

That one small "yes" was the first thread in a knot I would spend years trying to untangle. I believed I had been chosen by God and by my first boyfriend. I didn't realize I had just selected a path where, little by little, I would disappear.

"Neutrality helps the oppressor, never the victim."

~ Elie Wiesel

Chapter Three

The Night Before

Unease followed me like a shadow all day long before our wedding. I hadn't found a way to undo my "yes," and the consequences were unfolding fast.

The moment my parents learned we were getting married, they turned against my groom-to-be. He had once been my older brother's best friend, but that friendship dissolved the instant he chose me. Our house erupted into a storm of shouting and slamming doors. I felt trapped in a place I no longer recognized, let alone wanted to be.

The night before the wedding, my mother and I fought bitterly. I finally admitted that I didn't really want to get married; I just didn't feel safe at home anymore.

My father had come back from Vietnam a different man entirely, withdrawn and broken in ways no one dared acknowledge. He said nothing about the wedding. My mother, though, hounded me. *"Why? Why would you run off and marry?"* she cried, her hands flapping around her head like lost birds. Her face tightened with a hopelessness I had come to recognize. She detested the man I had chosen.

At last, I blurted out the truth I had carried for a few years, the unthinkable thing no daughter should ever have to say about her father. She chose not to believe me.[1] She said I must have dreamed it, and worse yet, that I must have wanted it. The shock hollowed me out. My body went cold, my mind going white around the edges.

Words that could never be unheard.

She stayed silent for a long moment. I studied her face, hoping for something, a softening, a change. When she finally spoke, her voice was cold. Backing out of the wedding wasn't an option. Too much money had been spent; too many people had been invited. It would shame the family. She didn't offer safety or love. She offered me exile.

So, I agreed to something I didn't actually want and chose her comfort over my own life. She wouldn't meet my eyes. She never thanked me for my "sacrifice," instead, she carried a quiet, simmering resentment I could never quite understand. She told me I could never come home. And I understood, with a clarity that hurt, that I wouldn't.

Wedding Night

I had imagined that being married would feel like arriving: a doorway into safety, into freedom, into finally having the permission to make my own choices. Maybe even into comforting love, everything I had hoped for. But when the door closed behind us, the room felt unfamiliar, and so did he.

We had fooled around before, petting, kissing, exploring like nervous young people who thought they were daring but were really trying to stay somewhat pure. When he had been drinking, the boundaries blurred even more, and I didn't have the kind of voice or confidence that protected what I wanted or didn't want.

The church said what we were doing was wrong, and the guilt always followed. But I told myself that once we were married, it would finally be good. Clean. Redeemed. And underneath it all was a quieter, crueler fear: *Who would ever want me now, after letting him touch me? Isn't that how girls become whores?*

But *This* Wasn't *That*

On our wedding night, I realized I had been imagining a man who didn't exist. His hands were not gentle. He reeked of alcohol. There was no tenderness, no sense that this was something shared or sacred. He had been drinking all day, and what he expected felt overwhelming and unfamiliar. I had thought it would be different. There was no time to say no. No room to hesitate. I didn't believe fear belonged here, yet my body was trembling with fear.

Something in me went very still. This wasn't being honored; this felt like being used. The popcorn-style, smoke-stained ceiling above me drifted farther and farther away. I stared at it, numb, while he moved through what he had been hungry for. I was in the room, but not really there. My mind slipped somewhere else, a safer place where everything went quiet, where I didn't have to know or feel or sort any of this. A place I already knew too well.

When it was over, I curled up small under the covers, the weight of it pressing into my chest. I lay still and quiet. He seemed satisfied and soon began to snore, but I felt emptied out, crying silent tears he would never notice. I told myself I loved him. I told myself this was what marriage was supposed to be, what we'd been taught to hope for, even if none of us really understood it.

This Was the Beginning

I didn't know then what would follow, but I had already learned something. Nothing felt right, and I didn't have the words to explain my feelings. My heart felt love for this Husband, but I was confused about his feelings for me. I had gotten myself into a fine mess.

With just one night, my new marriage felt wrong, with no words to explain it.

At dawn, while he slept, I slipped out to find a payphone. I knew I couldn't go home, yet a part of me still longed to crawl into my childhood bed and pretend none of this had happened. I wanted to believe that *home*, the idea of it, the hope of it, might still exist somewhere.

I swallowed my pride and lifted the cold black receiver of the hotel's pay phone. My fingers trembled as I fed quarters into the slot, one by one, unsure how many it would take. Each clink sounded too loud in the metal catch, echoing in the quiet hallway.

I didn't know what I was going to say. I just needed to hear her voice. The phone rang once. Twice. My breath caught. The world seemed to hold still with me. She answered. She answered!

For a moment, I felt like a child again, hoping she might somehow pull me back from what I had stepped into. I wanted to ask a thousand things: *Can I come home? Can I undo this? Can we pretend last night didn't happen? Can we forget what I told you about Dad? Can I start over?* My heart needed things from her I didn't have the words for.

She spoke first. Her voice was cold, sharp, dismissive, cutting.

I don't remember her exact words. I only remember the feeling of them, like a door slamming shut in my chest.

My mouth hung open. I had no words left in me.

While she was still speaking: harsh, punishing things I couldn't take in, I hung up. The change dropped into the tray at the bottom of the phone. I stared at it for a moment, listening to the quiet rattle.

Then I turned and walked away, leaving it behind.

It felt like another lock clicking shut. This would now be my life. **We moved into our first home.**

Note: I choose to believe my dad might have been a different man if he had not been so deeply corrupted by the events he was forced to endure, in his own life and the Vietnam War. This note is written not to erase the harm but to place it in the fuller truth of the time and of his life.

Chapter Four

Broken Dreams

After our one-night honeymoon, The Husband and I returned to the small apartment he had rented. I had no idea where I stood with my mother after the knife-edged phone call, but I still expected to go to work. We had started a lawn care company together. When she phoned to ask if I was coming in, relief rushed through me quickly, bright and fleeting.

Then he took it away.

I asked him to drive me (he still wouldn't let me drive his truck) but he told me I didn't need to work anymore; I wouldn't be working.[1] He'd support me now, he said. I would stay home and be a homemaker, the way the church said a good wife should.

Looking back, the fact that we hadn't talked about any of this before we married says everything about how young and unprepared we were. I didn't know he expected me to quit working. I don't think he meant for me to stop attending the community college I'd begun attending, but that day he gathered up my books, my hope, my future, and dumped them in the trash, telling me I didn't need an education.[2]

I remember standing there, too stunned to move, watching him do it. They weren't just books. They were hope. They were a doorway to a life I had barely begun to imagine, one where my mind and my thoughts might matter. And just like that, he threw them away.

He didn't yell or rage. He tossed the books away as if they were nothing, as if everything I'd been working toward meant nothing. I didn't fight. I had already lost other battles over things he didn't like: my clothes, my friends, almost everything I had carried with me into this marriage.[3]

It felt like a door closing, one more part of my life disappearing. I didn't cry in front of him. I just stood there in the kind of silence that burns, the kind that leaves ashes in your throat. It felt like watching my own future get carted off to the dump. I didn't have the words back then to say, "No, these are mine. This dream is mine."

I honestly thought I had signed away my rights the moment I said, "I do." Now, looking back, I think he was scared, not of the books, but of what they represented. Of whom I might become if I kept learning. Knowledge builds bridges, and he may have feared I'd find one and use it to leave.

Years later, when I watched *The Burning Bed,* with Farrah Fawcett, I was stunned. The woman in the film had lived through something uncannily close to my own experience. It felt as if Hollywood had placed a camera in our home and quietly filmed the parts of my life I'd never spoken aloud.

He made me call my mother to tell her I wouldn't be working anymore. He stood beside me like an angry parent, watching, listening, his glare controlling every word that left my mouth. I spoke in stiff, unnatural sentences, my voice barely my own. It was one of the hardest things I'd ever done, and it broke my heart.

I think she believed I had abandoned her and the business, that I was being lazy or selfish. I couldn't explain why I had to quit so suddenly. I didn't yet have the words to describe what was happening. I only knew I was trapped.

Inside, I suspected the person I had married was inhabited by both Jekyll and Hyde. If I could just love him more, maybe things would get better. I had been raised not to say no. Not to speak up. In my world, obedience was holiness, and silence was safety. The words I needed always came too late, after the door had closed, after the damage had settled like dust across the floor.

At the time, I believed The Husband had the right to instruct me. The church taught that the husband was the head of the wife. Only much later did I learn that the Greek word they built their teaching on doesn't mean authority alone, but can also mean source, like the headwaters of a river; there are other words for "to rule over." Yet the Christian churches chose the meaning that fit their narrative of power and control.[4]

I thought I was failing God if I disagreed. It took years to understand that saying yes to someone else again and again meant saying no to myself, losing pieces of who I was meant to become. All I knew then was that I had to quit something I loved and couldn't even tell my mother why. It broke something in me that took a long time to find again. I thought I was failing God if I disagreed.

As a newly married woman, I learned quickly that my "duty" meant doing whatever my husband told me to do. Each incident drove a deeper wedge between my mother and me. I wasn't allowed to visit her. I couldn't call when he was around. And I carried too much shame to admit she might have been right about him.

One of my mistakes had been trusting him with the truth about my dad. He couldn't understand why I'd want to visit parents who had hurt me, and I didn't have the words to explain it. They were all I had known, and in their complicated, broken way, I knew they had loved their children the only way they knew how.

My new life felt more restrictive and perilous than the one I had just escaped. By confiding in The Husband, I had unknowingly released our family's secret into the church. His father was a deacon, a role my dad had long hoped for but was never permitted to hold. When I learned that my parents had been hurt because of what my husband repeated, I understood why they let me drift away. If I had wanted to harm them, I would have gone to the authorities. I never imagined he would carry my family's pain into the church, tossing it into the chicken yard for others to peck apart.

I didn't know heartbreak could sound like silence. But that's what settled between all of us. I didn't really understand trust back then. I thought that if you whispered something to someone and asked them not to tell, it would stay just between you. I was learning secrets could be sharpened into tools, handed to people who would use them as a means of judgment. Years later, I realized just how far his whispering traveled, how deeply it affected my parents' standing. My dad never became the deacon he wanted to be, a strange mercy, given the darkness he was still living in at the time.

For years, I didn't know why my parents pulled away from me after I married. I carried the weight alone; certain I had caused it all. Now I see it differently. His words cost them their status. Maybe in their eyes, I cost them that, too.

Silence had always been my family's way of solving problems, a way they believed kept the peace. But silence doesn't heal anything; it only lets wounds deepen out of sight. Those unspoken struggles clung to them, to all of us, like crusty barnacles.

Note: Then vs. Now, The Law's Blind Spot
At the time these events took place in the 1970s and 80s, the law did not recognize what my husband did as criminal. A man could forbid his wife from working, throw away her schoolbooks, or intimidate her into obedience, and the justice system would dismiss it as "a marital matter." Today, these same actions would fall under California's definitions of **domestic abuse and coercive control**. *See endnotes and penal codes in the back of the book.*

Chapter Five

House of Non-Consent

I had openly refused to obey The Husband in the early years of the marriage. The consequence of this disobedience resulted in rape, or "not rape," depending on who I listened to about the subject.

My church taught me that a wife cannot be raped by her husband. A wife was to submit to all things, and they would expertly cite scriptures they believed substantiated their truths.

When I complained to our minister, he covered his slight smile with one hand and said, "It's not possible to be raped by your husband."

When I finally found the courage to tell my mother-in-law, she asked, "Did he hit you?"

"No," I answered.

"Then what are you complaining about?" she replied. Then, almost as an afterthought, she added, "I'm raped every day." Shocked, I looked into her sad, dark eyes, trying to fit this knowledge into God's plan.

A Husband, I was told, had a right to his wife's body at any time. Submission wasn't just expected; it was a duty. I felt crushed, ashamed that I had been wrong.

I felt mortified. I hadn't known this kind of behavior was so pervasive, so normalized in the shadows of women's lives. Her words, "I'm raped every day," echoed in my mind like a whispered confession dropped into a very deep well. I began to look at every man, both those in the church and the "worldly" men, differently after that.

Something shifted in me. I began to suspect that, behind closed doors, more than I could imagine, other women were being crushed under the same weight. I could not unhear her truth. And I couldn't help but wonder how many other husbands were demanding this, and how many wives were silencing themselves to survive.

Every man became a little more frightening. Sex no longer felt connected to love. It felt tarnished and sometimes dangerous, something to be endured.

Today, American society says sex must be consensual, or it is considered rape. (I wonder how the married church ladies navigate the difference today.)

We had eventually moved into a small, low-end, ground-floor apartment before my first son was born. The tiny space allowed chores to be completed within a couple of hours, leaving long, lonely days filled with empty time.

I wandered through the cramped rooms, isolated, with no one to call or visit. Hobbies from my teenage years, such as drawing and painting, felt out of place in this unfamiliar new life. Without money to go anywhere and facing the consequences of leaving home without permission, I stayed home, ensuring everything appeared perfect when The Husband returned.[1,2]

Motherhood had never crossed my mind, even as a dream. I had no experience babysitting or caring for infants, nor did I imagine myself as a mother. When my first son was born, this unfamiliar role felt insurmountable until my mother-in-law intervened. Her visits brought relief and gratitude as she guided me in basic baby care. I learned how to change diapers, nurse, and decode a baby's cries.

The Husband couldn't hide his disbelief at my lack of instinct. On our first morning home, I held the crying baby out to him, desperate for guidance.

"What am I supposed to do with this?" I asked, genuinely unsure. Without hesitation, he walked out the door, heading to work. "Figure it out," he threw over his shoulder.

From that moment on, the baby became my sole responsibility. His work, unwinding, and preparation for the next day's work took precedence. I don't remember him changing a diaper, taking a turn feeding the baby, or holding him very often. I'm sure he must have, but it seemed only a few times in between.

Although the baby's presence filled my days, a different loneliness shifted and took hold. I realized how little time I had left for myself. Life became all about fulfilling others' needs and demands. Everything was shrouded in sadness and despair. I didn't know it would be like this.

When my first son was several months old, my parents invited me on a trip to visit my brother in the Bay Area. I longed for this escape more than anything. Months of confinement in an apartment with a colicky baby and little outside contact had worn me thin.

The Husband considered my parents his enemies and forbade me from associating with them.[3] Despite their efforts to remain friendly and avoid conflict, he remained unbending in his opinion. There had been a history between them, with unresolved tension lurking beneath the surface.

The thought of the trip became a beacon for me after months of isolation, with only occasional visits and phone calls from my mother-in-law and a sympathetic neighbor. I craved a change of scenery.

Most days, I sat on the doorstep to calm my nerves while the baby cried inside. I had done everything I could think of to comfort him, but he insisted on crying and pushing away from me. I felt like a failure as a mom.

The neighbor, an older woman, often offered advice for soothing him, gently reminding me this phase wouldn't last forever. She was never invited in. The Husband would have disapproved.

Asking The Husband about the trip filled me with dread. I had learned the hard way that this marriage came with many unspoken rules and being with my parents violated a major one. We argued several times. But for once, I refused to back down.

I wouldn't call my parents to cancel. Early the following day, they arrived to pick up the baby, me, and the endless bags of supplies and accessories needed for traveling with an infant. The Husband sulked in the background, offering no help with the baby or bags, and embodying the mood of a petulant teenager.

The details of the trip's purpose have blurred over time. What mattered to me was getting away. All I cared about was leaving, even for a little while. Contact with my family had become almost nonexistent. None of us seemed to know how to connect. More than that, I didn't want anyone to see the cracks in my marriage or hear the unhappiness in my voice.

I feared their inevitable response: "Told you so."

Driving away from my life felt liberating, even surreal. For a fleeting moment, I imagined never returning, just keeping on the road. The thought brought a mix of hope and sorrow. Deep down, I knew there was nothing I'd miss back in that apartment.

I might have run if there hadn't been a baby. I would have packed what I could carry and vanished; maybe stood by a freeway with my thumb out, chasing something, anything other than this life.

But the baby changed everything. His tiny, perfect body, his helpless cries, his complete dependence on me . . . I was tethered. Not just by responsibility but by something deeper—*love*, an aching that bound him to me more tightly than any vow.

Even when I didn't know how to mother him, even when he cried and pulled away, and I didn't understand why, my heart stayed. I stayed. Babies don't get to choose their mothers, but mothers choose them daily, in all the moments we stay, even when we feel like running.

Sitting in the backseat of the car, with my son in his hand-me-down car seat beside me, I watched the world slip by. As the car rolled farther from the apartment, the thought of not going back flickered in my mind like a whispered dare. *What if I just... didn't return?* Not to run and vanish, but to live somewhere with my baby, separate from The Husband.

But my heart knew that was impossible. My mother had made it clear when she said I could never come back. Worse than the fear of starting over was the shame of proving her right, that the marriage she had disapproved of had become a cage.

Even if I tried to explain, what comfort could she offer now? She had already turned away once when I needed her the most; when I had entrusted her with a secret that tore at my soul. I couldn't survive being turned away like that again.

So, even though I was free for a moment, the road home still led me back to the place I didn't want to be.

On that trip, for the first time in months, I felt untethered from the endless concerns and suffocating worries of my married life. The escape brought a balm to my soul.

Deep down, I knew being away with my parents wasn't inherently wrong. I knew that. To The Husband, it broke a sacred rule, and I already anticipated the price I would pay later.

His anger had no predictable form. It manifested in ways I couldn't foresee. I would walk carefully, as always, on eggshells in my own home. Our marriage already felt like a battlefield of minor and significant skirmishes.

I came from a line of fiercely independent women, stubborn in their quiet ways. Though shaped by the church's rules of submission, my mother navigated life with strategies that bent the boundaries of those expectations.

Her mother, my grandmother, was the first divorcee in the small town where she lived, breaking the chain of an abusive husband she had at the time. I began to understand my parents' battles a little better.

Head of Household

This Husband, however, sought control over every facet of my existence. Whether driven by the church, his family's beliefs, or his swelling insecurities fueled by alcohol, he dictated what I wore, who I spoke to, where I went, and how I spent my days.[3]

His vision for my role confined me to the home, where I was expected to attend to his needs, care for the baby, and keep the house spotless. A part of me inside felt that this controlling behavior was unintentional, stemming from his underlying beliefs. But I felt like a possession.

Whenever I hesitantly mentioned it to the people I was allowed to be around, they said I should submit, try harder, and be less ungrateful. If I failed to be there to fetch him another beer from the refrigerator, I disrupted his entire sense of order.

The details of the day with my brother have faded from memory. I can't recall a moment, just the happiness and freedom that carried me through. Spending the day with my son and his grandparents provided a brief reprieve from the weight of my life. Oddly, they never asked me a single detail about my life, and I didn't volunteer conversation. As the car turned towards home, tension began coiling in my chest.

I felt the collapse of everything I enjoyed just hours earlier. That brief sense of freedom, of being myself again, was crushed under dread. The closer we came to home, the more I knew it was over.

We were returning not just to a place, but to a prison. Worse, I had no real defense. My life, my body, and even my hope no longer belonged to me. The prickling fear crept in, familiar and unrelenting.[4]

When we arrived home, he stood at the door like a giant, drunken bear. My heart sank at the sight of him swaying and glaring. I struggled to carry everything inside, my sleeping baby nestled in one arm, and the bags dangling awkwardly from the other.

His simmering anger charged the air, and the house seemed to vibrate with the weight of his rage. He watched me silently.

I tried to carry the joy from the trip inside, hoping he might soften and see how happy the outing had made me. But he stayed silent, his cold glare cut through the room like a knife.

I knew then it had already begun.

After laying my son in his crib, still soundly asleep from the long drive, I let the bags drop to the floor. My shoulders sagged under the weight of the inevitable. Stealing my nerves, I tipped the nursery door slightly closed and prepared to face what awaited.

The Husband grabbed the front of my blouse, pulling me to him. "You are never to do that again," he growled. His breath reeked of Cabernet Sauvignon wine, his favorite at the time. Even now, the scent of it churns my stomach.

With one rough motion, he twisted his fist in the fabric and shoved me backward into the other bedroom.[5] My blouse tore apart as he dragged me through the doorway. For a fleeting moment, I thought, *Really? He was finally going to do it; he intended to hit me.*

The idea almost felt like relief. If he hit me, I believed I could finally complain, legally.

I could finally be free.

We all thought abuse only "counted" if it left bruises from a beating. My mother-in-law believed it, as did other church ladies, and it was commonly accepted knowledge. No one talked about coercion, psychological control, power, and fear control. The church certainly didn't teach it.

I thought that if he hit me, it would finally count.

I could finally say something.

I could finally be free and leave.

His rage radiated through the room, paralyzing me. Fear locked my body. My fists balled uselessly at my sides.

He didn't hit me.

Instead, his hands ripped away the rest of my clothing with a fury that made his intent unmistakable. Each motion was deliberate, designed to dominate, to strip me of any sense of control.

More than my blouse was torn that day. Something deeper gave way, something unseen. The fabric of trust, already threadbare, split wide open. He meant to hurt me. He wanted to hurt me. In that moment, something inside me began to unravel.

"Don't you ever leave again to go out with *them*," he hissed, venom in every word. "Your place is here with me!"

He hurled more words, each one punctuated by his relentless anger.[6]

I got the message.

He shoved me onto the bed, his movements unrestrained and forceful. Somehow, in the chaos, he had stripped off his pants and underwear, his T-shirt still clinging to his chest.

I stared at the food stains on the front of it. A strange thought flickered in my mind: *He wants to have sex now, like this.* He reeked of alcohol and anger, his drunkenness adding a new layer of dread.

My eyes locked with his, searching for meaning, trying to grasp what he wanted. But I knew. He had already taught me that my role was to submit, no matter the time or circumstance. Submission, after all, was what the church preached and what he demanded. In the past, I had seen doctors for problems caused by his sexual attentions, appointments grudgingly permitted, even though the church discouraged medical visits.

He climbed onto the bed, flinging himself on top of me. His hands pinned my arms, tangling painfully in my waist-length blond hair. He anchored me to the mattress, leaving no room to move, no chance to escape. Without warning, he forced himself inside me with one violent shove.[7] Our eyes stayed locked, his full of rage, mine filled with resignation.

I tried to shift, desperate to lessen the pain, but his violence left no room for relief. [8, 9, 10]

My mind tried to retreat to the place it would go, the space that offered a fleeting escape from my dangerous world. But this time, I couldn't find it. Deep down, I told myself I deserved this, punishment for my disobedience.

He moved with pure, angry power, thrusting in rhythm with the insults ground out between clenched teeth. Each accusation, each claim of my disobedience, my unworthiness, landed like a strike, dripping with drunken spite.[11, 12]

His eyes, dark with malevolence, bore into mine, pinning me down as much as his weight did. I should have closed my eyes, should have turned away from his expression of contorted fury. But I didn't. I couldn't. That hate-filled passion flashing in his hazel eyes is forever stamped into my memory.

I stayed still, compliant, knowing any resistance would only escalate his rage. My gaze met his, defiant in its own quiet way, saying: *You'll never really have me.* Even drunk, he understood. I saw it in the flicker of recognition that crossed his face.

So, unless you said "No" and struggled, it is considered consent, right?

I didn't say no. I didn't fight. I knew it would only make things worse. But it felt like what I imagined rape would be. Even though I didn't fully understand the word, at the time, I knew this was something more than sex.

It was punishment.[13]

My penance for going against his will, for defying him. Fighting would have made it worse, and I understood that too well. Now, he had a new way to punish me whenever I fell short.

"I asked myself, Is this love, then?"

He often told me he loved me.

It felt like one of those freak rainstorms that strike without warning, violent turbulence, with tree-bending winds and stinging hail that pelted the skin, leaving bruises.

And then, as suddenly as it began, it ended.

The howling, the chaos, and the storm in my mind all gave way to silence, broken only by the drip, drip, drip of my lingering tears. He rolled off me, his drunken scent trailing behind, and pulled on his pants. His glare remained sharp and wordless as he left the darkened bedroom.

I lay there, curled up on my side, ignoring the tears of pain and of anger, of sorrow, or perhaps even relief.

It could have been much worse.

Yes, it definitely could have been worse.

What little I'd known about love and sex came from some illicit romance novels I had secretly read, stolen from beneath my mother's bed, before the waterbed had been installed. Those stories whispered of tenderness, passion, and mutual desire, in which the man seemed nearly to worship the woman.

This life, my reality, felt like the wrong story entirely.

Those books had lied.

What no one told us, what church never prepared me for, is that rape doesn't always come with screaming and beating. Sometimes, it comes wrapped in silence, with a shared bed and a marriage certificate. Sometimes it comes with the word 'love.'

I didn't fight because I knew it would make things worse. I didn't say "no" because I had learned that my "no" didn't count. That's what people struggle to understand: when a woman has been conditioned to believe her body isn't her own, that saying no is rebellion, that submission is holy, how can she honestly give consent?

This wasn't sex or love.

It *was* Control and Punishment.

Afterward, I spent years trying to convince myself it wasn't rape, because that's what I was told, but now I know silence does not equal consent.

I don't believe God would ask me to suffer like this in his name.

I thought about how much this so-called love can hurt. How deeply I hated this life, and how, in that moment, I hated being a woman. If it ever resembled *lovemaking* before, after that punishment, it became nothing more than duty, something to endure whenever and however he wanted it.

I stopped caring about making it special or meaningful. Choosing not to care at all felt safer for my heart. Whatever starry-eyed ideas I once held in my naivety had evaporated into the stale air of our apartment, leaving behind only emptiness.

Submission, I realized, carried a paradox. No matter how freely given, it required someone else to hold power. How could anything *offered up* under duress ever be considered a gift? If someone submits because they feel forced, what is the person in power really receiving?

My thoughts rebelled against the church's teachings, questioning how such a one-sided arrangement could ever be called love. Even now, I wonder, would God really find joy in people who obeyed only out of fear of hell, or hope for heaven?

If love or worship must be coerced or bribed, wouldn't it be empty? Meaningless? Whether offered to a God or a man, submission seemed to give nothing of real value.

Did The Husband's punishment of me earn him his place at the pearly gates, if they even exist? After all, he acted within his "husbandly rights."

When morning came, we never spoke of it. Can you believe that? Not one word. Did he even remember what happened? He acted as if nothing had occurred, so I followed his lead, burying my emotions deep.

But I never went anywhere with my family or anyone else for years.

There's a sorrow that lives in the heart of a girl who isn't believed. It starts as confusion: *Why don't they hear me?* And grows into something heavier, like shame.

When boys speak up, they're more readily taken seriously. When a girl cries out, especially about something as dark as harm, the world too often squints and says, *Are you sure? Did you misunderstand? Did you ask for it? What were you wearing?*

I learned early that my words didn't hold the same weight. Not in my family. Not in my church. When my mother didn't believe me, not even then, it wasn't just one betrayal; it reverberated every time someone else doubted me afterward. It taught me that if I were going to survive, I'd have to carry my truth and silence. That silence shaped the woman I became: careful with words, wary of trust, and slow to believe my own instincts.

The damage wasn't just the harm I endured; it was being told, in so many ways, that I didn't matter.

We had a way of moving past these terrible moments, pretending they never happened, like a bad dream dissolving into thin air. Yet they soaked into my skin, wrapping around my insides, and became a part of me.

I wondered how long I could carry all this loss and pain before I became too heavy to move. There was no room left for happiness, love, or even hope.

Perhaps I would just cease to exist. Dying seemed much more likely, I started to long for it.[14, 15]

Losing my vision of a better future, I began to think of death as an escape. I didn't feel made for this world. So far, no part of my life had offered joy, support, or partnership, only endless work, loneliness, and failure.

If it weren't for this moment of non-consent, it would have been another. Over time, a second son had started to grow inside of me. Did he come from a punishment? I sometimes wonder if he knew he deserved a different womb. A better family. One filled with hopes and dreams.

Just when I thought grief couldn't weigh me down further, sadness swelled, filling every corner of my mind and body. I later learned that sadness during pregnancy wasn't just an old wives' tale. Scientists have discovered that a mother's emotions are translated into chemical signals and hormones, which, in turn, affect the child.[16]

This baby was destined to carry more challenges than we knew how to handle. My second son entered the world with some congenital disabilities, his long arms and legs stretching out as if preparing to run from the very fears and sadness that haunted his mother.

In my mind, I couldn't escape the echo of Exodus 20:5: *"The sins of the fathers fall onto the children."* (I knew we would all bear the consequences.)

We eventually had to leave this house and move again to another one.

Note to Readers: If your life is reflecting any of these feelings or events, please seek counseling and trust your inner instincts. Refer to the resources at the back of this book or your city's domestic violence coalition for additional information.

Chapter Six

The Church that Raised Me

I loved all the rules of the church. They gave me a sense of knowing and safety, and by following them, I believed we could avoid the pitfalls of sin. I loved God's plan, and He (God was a he then) became my best friend when I was very young. I read the Bible regularly and took volumes of notes every Saturday at church. I was *all in*, even though it meant facing hard times within this church.

That was before the church betrayed us all.

Before I began to doubt, before the rules felt like chains, back when the holy days we celebrated still felt like fixed stars, shining gloriously in the night sky. They marked the passage of time and informed us of the next steps in worship. They felt inscribed onto my heart like tattoos.

I suffered bullying at school for my homemade clothes, the tight braids with ribbons that my mother forced me to wear, and my black plastic glasses. This was during the era of wild hair, ripped jeans, and miniskirts. Jeans were prohibited, and my dresses had to reach the knee to ensure proper modesty.

I never went to school dances. Never attended proms and would have been hard-pressed to find a boy who would even ask me. I had an overabundance of shyness, and my mother had told me I should be happy to be "quite plain and not ugly." But her words didn't help. My heart still felt broken from the rejection of the *worldly people* at school, even though I wasn't supposed to care. But I did care. There were people I cared about in the *world*, and I often wondered why they couldn't become chosen, too. What was God waiting for?

The church gave us great purpose and community, reminding us how special we were. (And who didn't want that!) The seven crucial holy days we kept developed a rhythm of worship throughout the year. Each was celebrated during a specific season and each represented part of God's plan for mankind. They were all right there in the Old Testament, with God's admonition to keep them forever.

Forever is such a long time.

Our Sabbath was strict, from Friday's sundown to Saturday's sundown; one could only study and look to God. There was to be no work and no seeking pleasure in other things. My brother and I couldn't participate in track meets, no matter how much our school begged our parents to let us attend. This was the cost of being one of God's chosen.

Weekends were such a relief to me when I was younger; at least I didn't have to attend school. Later, the life I became locked into meant the church was the only place I was allowed to go.

Heaven and hell weren't part of our belief system at that time. We waited for God's return and prayed that we would be among the 144,000 saved before the tribulation. Perhaps, though, we could die as faithful ones and be brought to life later. The other option? The lake of fire. Total annihilation for those who refuse God.

We didn't celebrate Christmas, sing carols, or look for Easter eggs. Those holidays were considered pagan. Halloween was the day I longed to celebrate the most, to dress up like somebody else, but we didn't celebrate it.

One Halloween, we were home alone later than usual. Our dad was off somewhere, where dads sometimes go to avoid being home, and my mom was at her part-time job. We were considered latchkey kids, kids who were left home alone and unattended.

We were supposed to keep the porch and inside lights off and go to the back of the house so kids wouldn't come knocking for candy. But my younger brother and I wanted *"in!"* We didn't have any candy, and I wanted to participate with something. So, we handed out dog bones and prunes to the kids who came to our door.

It was all great fun until the neighbors told our mother what we had done. I'm pretty sure we paid a price for that. *I was hoping God was busy elsewhere that night and hadn't seen our evil.*

Ministers guided our lives with passion. Some new converts were told to divorce if they were in what the church considered an "invalid" marriage. Our church had strict rules about marriage and who you could marry.

I can only imagine the amount of grief it must have caused those couples. I couldn't understand why they would have stayed and joined a church that asked them to do such a thing, until I recalled how special they made us all feel for being *one of God's chosen.*

We tithed ten percent to the church, saved ten percent for the festivals, and if you had enough, another ten percent was expected for widows and orphans, at certain times.

Most families seemed to follow the endless rules in their own way, choosing what mattered most to them. One family we were close to made the girls wait on their brothers, make their beds, prepare their meals, and treat their boys with even more elevated status than my family did.

Members followed the rules with varying degrees of enthusiasm. My father let us watch "Star Trek," a science fiction show that was said to be illegal by the broader circle of church members. My mother didn't wear her wigs and makeup to church because it wasn't allowed, but she did when she got a job when we were older. I wondered, as a child, wouldn't God notice?

I observed that women bore the brunt of these restrictions. No makeup, wigs, vanity-enhancing items, or pantyhose, which were only allowed when you were old enough to wear them.

This religion dominated our lives, with rules governing even what foods we could eat and what we could not. We followed the Old Testament rules about clean and unclean food, as outlined in Leviticus, as well as the guidelines for clothing and household items.

No Ouija boards were allowed, but conversely, no crosses typically worn by Christians were allowed, as they were considered pagan.

Healing, if needed, was to come through prayer and being anointed by your minister, *after repenting of the sin that likely caused the illness in the first place.* Doctors and vaccinations were discouraged. I never saw a scripture in the Bible that validated that. Still, since asking for anointing was the biblical way to deal with illness, people created their own ideas around other health services.

My church loosely mirrored Jewish tradition by endorsing circumcision on our sons around the eighth day, but there was no formal mandate or ritual enforcement tied to our faith, just a lot of church social pressure to do so. Looking back, I later learned that circumcision was not a medical necessity for most boys. Doctors today generally consider it optional, except in rare cases where a man might develop complications later in life.[1]

When I reflect on the broader behavior of church people I've experienced, it almost seemed that when other church people came over, they were ever so curious about what you had in your cupboards and home, and how you lived compared to how they lived. It became a game of spiritual one-upmanship.

Gossip was rampant. Overall, it appeared many church members tried to outdo each other in being "Christian," even as the minister told us we could not earn our way into God's grace. Indeed, it was a confusing message when there were so many required rules to live by.

In my young mind, everyone wanted to appear holier than everyone else, presenting themselves as religious in front of others, especially ministers, during the Sabbath or at festivals. But underneath, a current of judgment, gossip, and silent competition ran through us all.

I would see people praying at church one day, and then speaking cruelly about someone the next. It was easy to hear what went on. As a child, weaving between clumps of talking adults or just sitting in the bathroom stalls when no one knew I was in there, my ears grew red listening to the hen pecking against my mother and others.

It didn't seem to be about who had the kindest heart but who followed the rules better than the next. The hypocrisy clung like cling wrap everywhere.

Even as a girl, I sensed that some people were pretending to be good, but I didn't know what to think, as my parents did it too.

Surprising Things I learned Over 50 Years Later
Far into the future, after reaching incredible heights in membership and finances, and after convincing nearly 140,000 people (some say 150,000) that they were God's chosen people and the one true church, the said church tumbled from its self-made pedestal.[2]

Accused of being a cult and of gross misappropriation of funds, they were put into conservatorship by the state. They were even the subject of Mike Wallace's "60-Minutes" show![3]

By 1988, the church had lost 80% of its membership after admitting it was wrong, *wrong about a great many of its teachings*.[4] We were misled by teachings that ostracized us from the world, and convinced us we were chosen and special.

These teachings split couples apart by declaring their earlier marriages "invalid." Members were segregated by color regarding the activities they could participate in together. Whether it was spoken out loud or not, it was the truth. Most damaging of all, the church granted a license for abuse to thrive within marriages under the guise of the husband being the "Head of the Household."

I can't help but wonder how many of those little old ladies went without, while giving tithes of their small Social Security checks, and any income that they had, to the church. They lived in relative poverty, just like us.

The widow's mite and our poverty money paid for church leaders' fur coats, lavish homes, and automobiles; the proverbial lifestyle of the rich and famous. The often-used Bible verse about a rich man getting into heaven comes to mind: *"It is harder for a rich man to enter the kingdom of heaven than for a camel to go through the eye of a needle."* But conveniently, our church did not believe in heaven at the time.

Years later, I came across accounts of others who had lived through the same unraveling of our church in my Internet searches. As new leadership dismantled the very doctrines members had built their lives upon, the collapse was not just theological; it was deeply personal for many. People lost their sense of being chosen, their community, and in some cases, their families. Friendships were fractured, reputations were damaged, and the emotional toll ran deep. Some former members have spoken of lasting anxiety, spiritual trauma, and years of struggle, often requiring therapy to rebuild their sense of self. I even came across accounts with members in such despair that they considered ending their lives. It was a level of disorientation and heartbreak that few outside of it could fully see.

The church downsized, liquidated its properties, and underwent significant changes, including a name change. The shift in beliefs caused such widespread disillusionment that some members left to form splinter churches.[5] People scattered everywhere, like a handful of dropped pick-up sticks scattered across the floor.

The fracture of the church didn't mean the fear ended. I recall opening an email from another church acquaintance. It was from a person in one of the splinter groups. The message was chilling in its certainty: those of us who refused to join them (and therefore God) deserved to die.

It was just one person's words, but it carried the same echo of control and threat that I thought I had escaped by eventually falling away. That's what the church labeled you if you left: a fallen one, snatched up by Satan.

Then, even worse, the church had the gall to declare, "Okay, we *were* totally wrong about a bunch of stuff but we have fixed all that, and we have a new mainstream message. You can eat pork, celebrate Christmas, and have little baby Jesus cakes at Easter time now.

"How about you come back?"

And bring your money . . .

In my ignorance, the church had taken more than 27 years of my young life, teaching me their interpretation of the Bible, beliefs that shaped who I became. All that intense believing in their version of the truth, and all the suffering, was for nothing.

I was neither chosen nor special.

I was just someone who was fooled.

Now they had a new truth and a new name with the same Bible.[6] In a very tiny way, I am surprised at them, though. What church ever admits it was wrong, grossly, blatantly wrong? But a more wounded part of me, a sorrowful, broken piece of me, remains burned and leery of any religious group claiming they are the way to salvation, baby Jesus cakes, or not...

"It's awful what happens when people run out of money. They start thinking they're no good."

~ Barbara Kingsolver

Chapter Seven

House of No Money

Effects of Poverty

I stomped around in our old-fashioned bathtub, swirling dirty cloth diapers back and forth with my feet. A cloying scent of baby crap wrapped around the small room, mixing with the heat and steam, clinging to my clothes.

This is what I did because there was no working washer or money for the laundromat. Complaining and wishing for a different situation wouldn't put my babies in clean diapers. I didn't have a wash bucket. The bathroom sink was far too small for the number of diapers I had, and the kitchen sink, where I prepared food and washed dishes, was unthinkable.

My feet and ankles were red from the hot water, and I questioned whether they would ever be clean again. This became another thing I felt was impossible to share, a secret shame to add to all the others.

Having to Ask for Money

Two days after giving birth to Second Son, I had used up the pads the hospital had sent home. I dreaded asking The Husband for money. I wasn't allowed to work and asking him became my only way to meet even my most basic needs.

Whenever I asked, he wanted to know why I needed money. When I told him I was still bleeding and needed sanitary napkins, just as I did with First Son. He sighed and fussed as usual, but eventually handed me enough to buy a box.

I waited a moment, hoping he might offer to get them or drive me to the store. But he had already dismissed me, well into drinking and watching his favorite *John Wayne* rerun.

He had told me before that real men don't buy feminine hygiene products. They don't touch them. They don't take them off the store shelf. I had heard that lecture a few times.

So, I folded a washcloth, laid it in my panties, and walked out of the house, cradling my painful belly.

The March air was cool and clear, and for a moment, I stood there under the old shade trees, taking in the spring sun, just breathing. Our local market, which I had never walked to before, seemed farther away than the two long blocks it was.

Yes, the freedom of stepping out of the house felt intoxicating on the one hand, but as I walked further, nervousness crept in.

Being alone with myself rarely happened. The freedom to look around and think my own thoughts, not having to satisfy someone else's needs, felt indescribably wonderful. But the fear crept up as I walked through the neighborhood, conscious of being the minority white girl on the street.

Although I didn't understand the full scope of it at the time, there was real racial tension in the neighborhood where we lived, an area primarily made up of Black and Mexican families. As a white girl walking those streets alone, I felt eyes on me that weren't just about curiosity. They carried layers of history, injustice, and pain I hadn't yet learned to name.

Sacramento in the 1980s still bore the weight of its segregated past, and I was an outsider walking through wounds I couldn't see, much less understand. I didn't blame them for the stares; I didn't know how to live inside that divide.[1,2]

I felt unsettled by the town and the noise of the traffic. Most cars crawled along with windows down, their favorite radio stations blaring, a clamorous jumble of sound. Dark arms would dangle out of car windows, flicking cigarette ashes with their fingertips. Their eyes, when they saw me, felt heavy. Sometimes, men hooted and catcalled.

I tried not to look; I just counted the cracks in the sidewalk as I walked.

Some people scared me with their stares, mismatched clothes, shambling walk, and loitering positions. These were the broken ones, the lost ones, homeless or nearly so, entangled in drugs, alcohol, or simply the pain of being alive. Trash and wild weeds littered the entire area along the sidewalks and alleyways. No one seemed to love this place.

This place represented poverty everywhere you looked.

This is where we lived.

"Just two blocks," I whispered to myself, trying to look, and yet not look, at everything around me. Sweat beaded on my forehead, and I felt faint, my heart swirling in my chest. I felt sick. The terror of imagining myself throwing up in public, in front of God and everyone, caused me to stop and pant.

At the crosswalk light, I felt the blood seeping out of me, picturing it trailing down my leg, adding to my shame. I quickly found what I needed at the store and looked for a female checker. There wasn't one, so I went to the shortest line. Embarrassment at buying the pads caused my cheeks to pinken. My breasts tingled with a warning that milk would soon follow.

So much grief existed in being a woman.

I noticed that male checkers didn't hesitate to touch the box, even bagging it for me without flinching. I guess it's different if you're paid to handle them.

Someone nearby asked me if I was okay, but I couldn't answer. If I opened my mouth, there's no telling what might have tumbled out.

It was a slow walk home, and I dreaded going back. Yet I longed to lie down, curl up with my Second Son, nurse him, and sleep. Staying away for too long allowed the chaos of my thoughts to creep up on me, just as they did at night when I lay down, listening to my family sleep.

Would someone who loved you ask you to walk to the market only two days after giving birth? I thought about those old stories we'd heard since the Vietnam War, women in the rice paddies giving birth and then standing up to work again. Maybe he believed that was normal. But my body knew better.

Maybe it was a guy thing? Are these two blocks really considered nothing? Bitterness, anger, and shame bubbled up inside me. These feelings followed me everywhere like shadows.

I was sure everyone saw my embarrassment at how I lived, and the shame of not being a good enough wife to be treated better. I was disappointing God with these feelings, completely missing the beatitudes of love in the Bible by a mile. My thoughts against The Husband made me unholy, and again, I wasn't good enough.

Asking for money gave me so much pain. It felt like swallowing glass shards, like groveling for something not deserved. It crushed my soul. I hated it and resolved that someday, I would never have to ask anyone for money again.

That I even had to ask left me feeling bewildered. I couldn't earn or have my own money, so how else would I meet my needs?

When I came into the house, The Husband asked for the receipt, looked it over, and then held out his hand. Confused, I stared at him.

"The change," he said, arching an eyebrow, rubbing his thumb and two fingers together.[3]

It was just loose change and a bill, but I felt a subtle loss of power when I pulled it from my pocket.

"My mom used to steal money like that when she went grocery shopping. She didn't give Dad back the change," he said, while glaring at me, letting the words sink in. "I won't have that in my home," and then more sternly, "You just know that."

I wasn't even worth loose change.

The Stolen Shoe Money

After my first son had been born, my mother tucked twenty dollars into my purse for me to buy his first pair of shoes. She rarely saw the baby or visited, but she wanted to buy his first pair of shoes. After my second baby, she came over, took one look at him sleeping, never held him, said "Yep, looks like a baby," and left no money for his shoes. Not that I expected it, but it reminded me of the shoe money she had given me for First Son. That money had stayed hidden, a precious thing.

I don't know how The Husband found out about the money, or how many times he might have checked my wallet, as if I'd somehow earned money secretly. But he had taken it and bought himself a bottle.[4]

Filled with rage when I found the money missing, I pushed back, glaring at him. Fury burned in my words as I told him he had no right to EVER go through my purse. That money was not his; it had been a gift from my mother for First Son's shoes.

He eventually returned the money, but both of us knew something had radically shifted in our relationship. I had finally pushed back with a vehemence that startled us both.

Winning didn't feel like a victory. It didn't give me back my power. It didn't make anything equal or fair.

What it meant was that, for once, I said something firm and loud, and he backed down. That was new. It was like a broader crack in our little marital teacup.

He still held the power. He still controlled the money, the decisions, the tone of our home. But he knew something in me had changed. I had spoken. I had stood up for something.

It didn't fix anything, but it marked the beginning of a quiet, internal shift. The kind of shift that might take time to rise, but it never stops once it's begun.

The Husband looked at me with even more disappointment and suspicion. My heartbreak that he would steal from me added to my unhappiness about him. He always jokingly said, "What was his was his, and what was mine was also his." And then he'd laugh loudly.

It's Easier Not to Want

I learned not to want things. Instead, I filled a need by inventing solutions, creating what I could with my hands, or simply learning to do without. The humiliation of asking for money ran too deep, especially when it was sometimes turned down.[5]

Our church had a thrift store in a member's garage, where I could find baby clothes for free. My sister-in-law generously sent us her son's outgrown clothing, which helped my sons. Finding clothes that fit me was challenging because I was a tall, thin girl.

My clothing was primarily thrift store wear, often sourced from church donations and cast-off items from others, particularly maternity clothing. I had never been inside a hair salon, let alone a nail salon, or a clothing store, just for me.

When the babies started coming, it became increasingly difficult to find time to sit down and sew or work on other projects that could improve my life. There was enough to do just trying to keep up with life. If I couldn't fix it, refurbish it, or make it, we just went without.

Years later, when I finally earned enough to buy my own things, I graduated from thrift stores to actual stores, marveling at the idea of clothes that didn't need to be altered or that no one else had ever worn.

The Husband had started his own business before we were married. He was full of hopes and dreams for it, I was sure. His father had trained him to be a glazer. I think he was probably very good at the physical work, but running a business and doing the trade are two different things.

The Husband seemed to be constantly stressed, and drinking seemed to be the only thing that brought him peace. He lost that business or quit, I'm not entirely sure which, because he didn't discuss it with me, but later he began working at his dad's glazing business.

Some sons can work with their fathers, and life is good, but for The Husband, the partnership also seemed particularly stressful. Some days, when the alcohol didn't help, he would come home in rare form spouting anger and criticism.,

Nothing we did could settle him down. We had to wait until he drank enough to pass out before we could exhale our relief and tiptoe about our lives. Perhaps he felt as unhappy with his end in life as I felt. Maybe he discovered that having what he thought he wanted was less satisfying than the wanting of it.

He was the one who had wished for marriage and talked of having children. He did not speak with me about his feelings, so I could only guess. Unlike some women, I did not ask for children. I did not believe our home was a good place for them, but they came anyway, despite my best efforts at birth control.

Even so, they became the precious jewels that shone in my life. My heart was mesmerized by the tiny fingers and toes I kissed. Their soft heads lay in the crook of my arm as they looked into my eyes while nursing, and we stared, deeply lost in each other's gaze.

They were why I lived.

We eventually had to leave this house and move again to another one.

Note to Readers: If your life is reflecting any of these feelings or events, please seek counseling and trust your inner instincts. Refer to the resources at the back of this book or your city's domestic violence coalition for additional information.

Moving Always Moving

We moved a lot. Sometimes it was because we were changing jobs, and sometimes we outgrew the space in our home. And sometimes, when you are poor, the lack of affordable home choices decides for you.

In between rentals, we occasionally stayed with The Husband's parents. We strained their lifestyle, and The Husband's style was strained in turn, as he had to drink less. His mother ran a daycare from her home, and adding my children to the mix meant more work and stress for her.

For a while, we even lived with my older brother. That was where I tried to run away the second time. The first time was in Oregon, where we had moved into a house in the middle of a mint field. Each time I had to go back, there was nowhere to go. There was no money, no friends, no family. Once the first baby arrived, I felt cemented in place.

It felt like we never had a place to call our own. Always renters, always temporary.

Each time we moved, it felt like a new beginning, at least for a moment. I packed every box and bag. I had to decide what to keep, what to discard, and which delicate items I wanted to move myself, since I didn't trust The Husband not to ruin them.

I didn't have friends who could help. I certainly couldn't ask my parents, and my in-law relatives were busy with their own lives. I'm sure they must have helped, even fixed things at times, but the overarching feeling I carried was being in this alone, over and over again.

I scrubbed out cupboards, closets, and floors until my fingers ached. I patched holes in the walls that the kids and I hadn't made. I swept out every last corner of each old place with a tired kind of reverence, as if the broom might somehow sweep away the past, too.

No matter how we found the places we moved into, I always left them in better and cleaner condition.

The Husband came with friends from his work and carried boxes to the truck; that part he did. But the rest: sorting, boxing, cleaning, organizing, the endless questions of *Where does this go?* and *How should we set this up?* were my job. It all fell to me, even with babies clinging to my legs or crying in a nearby room, puzzled at why their things kept being moved here and there.

There was no complaining allowed. At least not out loud.

Most of the houses we moved to had only one bedroom for our children to share. It was what we could afford. It wasn't so difficult when they were younger, since they didn't have many personal belongings. What mattered most was having a yard where they could run off their ceaseless energy.

This was back before computers, Xboxes, and other devices kept kids indoors, back when children actually played outside.

I homeschooled in the early days, but later, when they entered public school, moving from school to school made things hard on the boys. They were unaccustomed to being out in the world and facing the challenges it presented. None of them played team sports or joined school clubs; they preferred each other's company and whatever yard we happened to have at the time.

Because each new house brought a flicker of hope, I'd whisper a lie to myself while unpacking the same belongings into a new layout: *Maybe this one will be different. Maybe this is the house where The Husband will change, be happy, and then we could be happy too. Perhaps it was just the cramped space, the noise, the stress of the last home. Probably in this larger place, we'll find peace.*

But the walls didn't matter.

No matter how much square footage we gained, we carried the same silence, the same anger, the same rules and roles from house to house, like a dark shadow that refused to lift.

*"One cannot think well, love well, sleep well,
if one has not dined well."*

~Virginia Woolf

Chapter Eight

House of Hunger

I put the loudly quacking duck in a large black garbage bag. My heart tripped over itself as my mind clouded in fear, trying not to think, yet carrying terrible remorse for the deed I was about to do.

Tears ran down my face and dripped off my nose as I dug a small hole in the flower bed for the remaining parts of the duck we could not eat. I smeared them away with my free arm, the other one still supporting the weight of the knife.

This new nightmare started because we had no food except for some white rice. We had been eating it daily for a few days, at all three meals. We also had some margarine, rationed between my pregnant self and my two young boys. That morning, the boys cried and refused to eat yet another bowl of rice.

You might say that, if we were truly hungry enough, we would have eaten it. But I had learned a puzzling truth: hunger is not just a physical pain; it drags along a distinct kind of fatigue.

Food is pivotal in the joy of life, if you're lucky. We saw magazine covers and TV commercials with unbelievable dishes, and beautiful people gathered around tables we could only imagine. We were so tired. A knot of hunger was in our bellies and minds, and more rice couldn't fix it. We smelled the neighborhood barbecues; the scent of a pumpkin pie in the breeze; the waft of someone's morning cinnamon toast and coffee.

The unfairness of it all.

I could not fully understand why we did not qualify to shop, buy, and eat like other people. Did God mean to starve his *Chosen Persons*? If I tried to mention that we had no food to eat (in the least upsetting way possible), The Husband would lash out and rage, "What do you want me to do about it? I go to work every damn day— there is JUST not enough money! You're soooo damn ungrateful!"[1]

There were rules in this marriage of who was to do what. For me to ask for food, or anything really, was touchy business.

Taking on any aspects of his role was even more touchy.

According to my church, I knew what I had planned crossed a line. (1st Timothy 2:12: *The whole woman cannot teach, nor usurp authority over a man, but should be silent.*) One of my jobs became manifesting meals, apparently from nothing. I was expected to be all the things a woman is told to be in the Bible, "a virtuous woman." (In some translations, Proverbs describes a virtuous woman as a noble, gracious, diligent, and loving woman, among other things. All the virtues she practices aim to improve her husband's life, teach her children, and serve God. In this way, she faithfully honors and pleases her husband.) These were the things I was brought up to believe in. I tried, I really, *really* tried.

The Husband met his dad most days to go to work with him. They often ate many of their meals out at restaurants. It was only on the weekends that he might have noticed the lack of food in the cupboards. Having his blackberry brandy became much more critical, and there was no reasoning with him once he started drinking.

We never had any steady money for food at this time, yet there always seemed to be enough for another bottle. It was the secret elephant in the room we all tiptoed around. It all remained impossibly confusing, heartbreaking, and exhausting. Did I find myself resentful? Yes. But I learned the hard way not to speak of it.[2,3]

What a fine mess I found myself in. The Husband had quit going to church, and now I lived with an unbeliever. Our marriage was unequally yoked. Mom's words echoed in my mind: "If you marry him, you can't ever come back home," even though she told me to marry in the end. And her favorite refrain, said to me later in life, "You made your bed and now lie in it."

But there I was still in the old-fashioned kitchen of our rented home. I stared at the bowls on the table. I could not bring myself to eat more of that rice. I could not even shame my sons into it. They would eventually come back to the sticky grains in their bowls, and so would I, accepting anything to relieve the hunger.

But I had hatched this plan for a delicious meal in my mind, and so I found myself preparing for the first step.

The boys were finally down for naps. I needed them to stay asleep so they wouldn't witness this crime. Some ducks had wandered into our backyard a while back and had become our "pets," sort of. I can't tell you how it happened, or whether we fed them, but about three had just shown up one day, free to come and go.

I had easily picked up the male duck, who now writhed in my hands. The shimmering beauty of his feathers and his knowing eyes made me bag him. I couldn't stand to look at what I was about to do.

I slipped the knife into the bag too, trying to locate his neck in his struggles. Holding my breath while pressing his body hard to the ground, steeling myself. I sawed through his neck with that terrible excuse for a kitchen knife, just as I had seen my "farmer" mom do years ago with her chickens.

Before that moment, his eyes had been so knowing, staring into mine, somehow aware of his impending death. Sobbing and silently thanking him for his life, mortified over what I had done. I vowed to find a way for us to escape this hunger someday.

If you have never taken a life, I can tell you it cracks your soul a bit. It's been years, and the memory remains tucked in a deep corner of my mind.

Back then, in that backyard, my chest seized tight, so drenched in fear over what I was doing, that I rocked back on my heels, holding the duck down inside the bag until his life ebbed away. I sobbed even harder for the choices that had led me to that moment.

His thrashing struggles surprised me, the intensity of his desire to live. Raised as a meat-eater, I had processed chickens with my mother, but she was always the one who took their lives. I had often fished, descaled, and cleaned them. But I had never killed any other animal.

I can tell you that if you did have to kill your own meat, you would pick the bones clean and throw nothing away. You would smell the coppery scent of blood, feel the life leave beneath your fingers, and feel its loss for your gain. You would come to understand that there should be reverence for that—an honor for its life.

It would be shameful to waste even a scrap.

Mamma Marks

I chilled under the sweat on my skin and brought out his limp body, staring at what I had done. At that moment, my thoughts cleared, slipping past our hunger and into the broader fear: *What would The Husband do if he found out?*

Not long before, I had been "punished" for riding a bike down to Mama Marks's food bank to get food.[4] I was punished both for leaving my sons with our neighbor, a woman who had silently befriended me, and even worse, for bringing home food, which He claimed was *his* job to provide.[5, 6]

(Never mind that there wasn't anything to eat in the house.)

I had ridden the bike through Del Paso Heights to Mama Marks and stood there, the only white girl for blocks, asking her if I could help or do something in exchange for food for my boys. She laughed a full belly laugh, her dark eyes flashing, and she looked me up and down, just as the other workers were doing.

Maybe they saw my whiteness first. That much was obvious, and in those streets, I stuck out like an apology no one had asked for. Maybe I looked pathetic, skinny, and pregnant. Perhaps she thought it funny that I was here visiting her food bank. Uncomfortable and ashamed, essentially begging, I searched the ground rather than their faces.

Whatever she saw, she caught the scent of my desperation and took pity on me. She told me to get in line, and I could return and work at another time. Relief washed over me, mixed with humiliation because she hadn't allowed me to earn it. But the hope of some meals kept me from falling apart.

Helpers handed out sacks, one per person. I nested mine in a salvaged baby seat that I had cleaned up and modified to fit on the bike. My hand slipped back every so often to feel if it was still there as I pedaled. But as I drew closer to home, dread rose like a tide. I knew I had crossed one of his invisible lines.

I can't say, after all these years, what we got that day in the bag, or whether it was worth the consequences. But the warm feeling of solving a problem alone, and the bravery I showed that day, have never left me. I felt sure of my right to do this as a mother.

He prevented me from going to the food bank again, something I later discovered might constitute a form of false imprisonment.[7] His control over every aspect of my life, including when and how I could feed my children, was suffocating.

So, if "bringing home the bacon" from a poverty food bank was stepping way outside my enforced role, what would He think of this, me killing the duck?

Now, standing in the backyard, my fear grew quickly, suffocating my thoughts. Before I could reason anything out, I stuffed the dead duck back into the garbage bag, shoved everything into the hole, and covered dirt over it with frantic, quick sweeps of my hands.

As if it had never happened.

As if I could pretend I had not felt its shudders.

As if I could undo the moment.

Back in my house, I paced the floors, gasping for air, my heart like a fluttering hummingbird in my chest. I tried to scrub away the blood and dirt, still tearing up, frustrated beyond my understanding. I had only wanted to see my boys enjoy a real meal, with the scent of roasting meat and the relief of flavor after days of rice.

Why hadn't I thought this out better? Why hadn't I considered what He might think?

I sat in the kitchen chair, rocking back and forth, trying to tame my panic. Every possible solution required lying, something that felt sinful to me and required more skill than I possessed. Lying begets lying, then more lying, until it tangles into knots, and what has my church taught me about that?

Lying was a *written-in-stone* sin.

So, what should I do?

Pretend I didn't know what happened to the duck?

Say nothing and let it rot in the ground?

Cook it and face him, come hell or high water?

As my stomach pained, I thought of the life I had taken, now about to be wasted in a hole in the ground. That became the greatest crime in my mind.

To waste a life felt like yet another shame.

I flew back outside, dug out the duck, and carried it to the back porch. It hadn't spoiled; not enough time had passed. I plucked the feathers into the bag, trying to keep everything hidden. Our church taught that animals had to be bled out to be "clean to eat." The duck had bled a lot…was it enough? I couldn't think about that now. Nap times never lasted long.

If you have never plucked and gutted a bird while pregnant, I can tell you it takes all your resolve not to heave. The duck's body had a fusty, earthy, wet scent, with warmth still lingering. I just kept thinking about the goal, a real meal, and how happy my sons might be.

A duck is like a chicken, right?

I learned they are not.

My oldest boy, who was maybe five years old at the time, caught me rinsing the bird in the kitchen sink. His eyes widened, the eyes of an innocent who had stumbled onto a crime scene. When understanding flitted across his face, he became so upset that he cried out. His brother woke, and soon the two boys stared at me, horrified, while guilty feathers clung to my front. I had begun to burn off pins and hairs over the gas stove flame, blood oozing from the mangled neck onto the sideboard.

They tried to puzzle out what I was doing into a reasonable story in their young minds. It went from bad to worse.

I told them I was cooking this duck to help them not be so hungry. It would be like having chicken.

"One of *our* ducks?" my oldest son asked, and I watched my plan crumble.

They swore they would not eat any of it—at all—EVER! My oldest led the charge, and the younger was quick to follow. They stayed in their bedroom, avoiding me and the kitchen for a long while.

I knew they were hungry, and now they were sad and angry, too.

I cried even more while finishing the bird for baking. It seems that what my husband always said was true: *I never did anything right.* Ducks are not chickens. They're fattier, tougher, with no drumsticks to speak of.

There was no one to call, no one to pour out my sadness to. So,

I hardened myself to the task and filled the house with the aroma of roasted duck to the pains of all our stomachs. It came out mostly burnt and blackened due to my inexperience; its stumpy legs pointed stiffly upward.

Even pregnant, even feeling starved, I could not eat it. The picture of my sons' faces, glowering at me in disbelief, was too painful. When the duck cooled, I put it in the refrigerator.

Later, The Husband ate it, no questions asked, while my sons and I ate rice. I don't remember if I was "punished" for the killing or not. Nothing more could top the memory of the boy's dislike of me in that moment.

I never touched the other ducks. I don't remember what became of them. I think they disappeared one day.

Killing it became one more terrible memory, one I was disgusted with myself for creating.

Each day rolled on, and there was always another crisis to be weathered. Hunger colored my life in drab grays, stretching each day longer and longer. I began dreaming about the meals of my childhood. I imagined standing in my mom's home, one entire room filled with her home-canned goods. There were shelves of peaches, pears, apples, potatoes, and tomatoes, freezers full of meat, and her mother's old crocks brimmed with fermenting cabbage. She even kept chickens in the backyard, laying eggs. She had planted a small garden plot in her backyard, nestled in the suburbs, steadily growing more food. Her hands blessed us all.

Not long after the duck incident, desperation grew. One day, The Husband angrily commented on the lack of good meals and accused me of not learning how to cook.

"You always make the same stuff! No wonder no one wants to eat it!" he growled with drunken disdain. But I had so little to work with, how could I cook delicious food?

I stood there shaking, not just from fear but from frustration and helplessness. His spending on alcohol while berating me for basic survival costs felt like an unending cycle. Even knowing that, I felt stymied about how to have a different life. By God's rules, I could not simply leave him.

The burning question was: where would I go if I did?

The culmination of these moments burned something into me: if I wanted my children and myself to survive, I would have to step outside the rules he built around us. His control and neglect were no longer just painful; they were beginning to look like something else, something wrong in a way I couldn't yet name.

I didn't have the language then; I hadn't read the books, learned the terminology, or even understood the laws. All I had was the sharp, rising certainty: what was happening in our home wasn't just cruel, it was dangerous.

One day, I told myself I would understand exactly what I was living in. And one day, I would find the way out.

Before hunger became a constant shadow in my married life, I came from a world where shelves were always full, where food wasn't a question or a prayer. To understand the shock of those empty cupboards, you have to understand the home I came from.

Before I Came "To Lie in My Bed"

I grew up in a comfortable middle-class family, with a "frustrated farmer mom," a military dad, and two brothers, one older and one younger. Mom longed for a farm her whole life, but being married to an army man meant moving every few years and starting gardens she could never keep.

That didn't stop her. She "rented" neighbors' yards, both front and back, planting vegetables wherever she could coax food from the soil.

She shared everything she grew. We always had more than enough.

Dad built a room inside our two-car garage, with shelves lining the walls, filled with rows upon rows of jars holding peaches, tomatoes, pears, sauerkraut, and whatever else Mom had canned, pickled, or fermented that season. She was doing organic farming and prepping decades before it had a name.

My favorite after-school snack was simple: open a quart of her canned peaches, whip fresh cream from the raw milk she bought "with a wink" from a local dairy farmer (sold *legally* for animals, but shared with pets so as not to "break the law") and dig in. We rarely bought packaged food. Soda and white-flour treats were reserved for camping trips, where they arrived like contraband delights.

Mom made soap, candles, and some of our clothing; she even cut our hair. Back then, I had no idea how blessed we were, how much work it took to keep a family fed in that way.

One day, she packed bags of food into the car and drove us far into farm country to deliver supplies to another church family. There, I was gob-smacked with dirt-poor poverty, found right here in America, just an hour or so drive from our cupboards of plenty.

That's when I first recognized poverty.

Six people lived in a single-room shanty. Two stained mattresses sat on the floor against opposite walls, filling most of the space. A tiny counter and an old utility sink served as their kitchen. A rope across the room held two limp sheets, trying to split the space into "rooms," a fragile attempt at privacy.

This couldn't be their real house...could it?

It wasn't a home to my eyes. It was something I couldn't put a name to. They were not expecting company. I felt awkward as they stared at me, and I stared at them, both sides of us at a loss for words.

Obviously, the whole family slept there and lived there. They accepted the sacks of food, maybe a bit awkwardly, I couldn't be sure. I was ready to go back outside, unsure of what to say, uncertain of what to look at.

The mother whispered with mine. We continued to stare at each other. They accepted the food with an awkwardness I didn't yet understand. I felt stunned into silence on the drive home. Mom never explained it. She wasn't a talker. She simply acted, and I followed.

Seeing that family again at church, scrubbed up, looking almost like everyone else, haunted me. I knew their secret. I knew how they slept, how they lived. I didn't speak of it to anyone.

As a teenager, I resented my parents for their strict rules and hypo-crisies, but in those moments, delivering food without an audience, without praise, I felt a deep, hidden pride in my mom. She lived what the church preached: caring for others quietly, without fanfare.

Even then, my dad would mock her efforts, wanting her to "relax and party more," yet he happily ate every meal she made and basked in the admiration of visitors when they praised her shelves of food. He took credit for work he never touched. That was its own kind of hunger, too.

All of that abundance, all of her quiet strength, lived inside me when I became a wife and mother, and it made the reality of my marriage and the cupboards I now stared into feel even more unthinkable.

The Enemy Was Inside Our Home

I knew my parents were considered the enemy by The Husband, and although I disagreed, it was a disagreement I could not speak of. It became an issue we danced carefully around, or at least I did. The boys and I did not visit my parents very often.

On the rare occasions when I saw my mom, she skillfully managed to be around the disagreeable Husband without making the situation worse. I knew she disliked him, yet she did nothing he could point to as interfering with his God-given right to rule his home, except maybe once.

In her defense, she had a good reason.

Mom stepped in when I had to attend a Lamaze class for the birth of my third son. The Husband was angry that he had to drive me there and, mostly, that he had to attend the class or else we could not do the cheaper "home birth in hospital" option. At this home, I did not yet have my own car, and he never allowed me to drive his truck or renew my license.[8]

He was also mad, as it turned out, that my mother was the only one available to watch the boys while we went to class. She never visited as a rule, and he didn't allow me to consort with her, as she and my dad were still the "enemy."

Enemies, I later realized, were "those people" who disliked my husband and might persuade me to leave him if given the chance. Nearly everyone became an enemy.

That night, his anger radiated from him in waves, his eyes flicking around as he searched for a target, any target, that might quench his rage.

How to Hide the Empty Cupboards

Before my mother came over, I had thought long and hard about avoiding letting her see the shame of having no food. So, I devised a plan to steal from my neighbors' trash cans.

(And just so you know, I had reasoned that it wasn't really stealing, as I would put it all back there later.)

I took an empty box of mac and cheese, a bread bag, empty cans, whatever I could find. First, I cleaned them up and put them on my shelves to make it look like I had food. I even stuffed the bread bag with brown paper sacks, so it almost looked full of bread if you didn't look too closely.

I had a strange sense of pride in my deception. This would save me from shame. Nothing could be done about the refrigerator, though; it mainly remained empty.

When we came back later that night, my mom left quickly as The Husband and I came in after the class. She was not one to stay around where she felt unwelcome, and she had to work the next day. The boys were all sound asleep in their beds.

Isn't it funny how, even when your refrigerator is empty, you still have that strange habit of opening it? When I pulled it open, it was filled with food, meats, milk, cheeses, and other items. In shock, I slammed it closed and stood there. Then, a moment later, I pulled it open again.

Yes, it was still full of food.

All I felt was fear. What had she done?

I peeked in the cupboard and saw that all my fake food had been replaced with real food! I started to tremble and could not catch my breath.

As I stood at the cupboards, my husband walked past me to get ice for his latest drink and bellowed from the pantry. "Who put this food in here!" He had been suffering for a fight all night, and now was his chance. Bad enough, he had to leave his drink and sofa to attend a birth class and put up with enemies in his house. Now, they had emasculated him by insinuating he could not feed us.

Frightening when in a rage, he confronted me as if I had a hand in it! (He did not know about my fake food plan, and it would have made it worse if he did.) When he got this way, his rage seemed to shatter the safety of our home, and I just wanted to calm him, afraid of what he might do.[9]

I just wanted all of this to go away.

He found the grocery sacks and began repacking them with the contents of the fridge, all the while glaring at me and saying the worst things he could imagine about me, my family, and how wrong we all were. In disbelief, I saw the food being carelessly tossed back into the bags.

He intended to drive over and drop it on Mom's doorstep, and he demanded I call her right now to tell her. I was supposed to support his righteous anger; to prove we didn't need it. I cried and refused, cried from fear and grief at seeing the food going away, seeing the food there, to begin with, and seeing that my fake food plan had not worked.

Apparently, my sons complained of hunger, and she had found nothing to feed them. She was probably shocked and worried. (I had fed them a dinner of Hamburger Helper.) She had loaded them into the car and taken them to the market just two blocks away. I don't know how she managed without baby car seats or knowing where to go, but things like that never stopped her.

I felt terrible that she had spent the money and now knew how I was living. Later, I lay in bed thinking about the food that I had eventually put quietly back after he had ranted and drank himself into a stupor, too drunk and too tired to drive the long distance back to my mom's.

I was painfully hungry but could not get out of bed to eat. When he was this drunk and this unreasonable, it would have been a stupid, dangerous thing to.[10]

Tears tracked down the sides of my face, disappearing into the pillow. I needed to be more like my mom. I needed to obtain food, grow it, and store it on shelves, filling my home with it. I suddenly thought of the family my mom had taken food to so long ago, when I was a teen.

I wondered if they felt as awkward getting the food we had brought them as I did at the food bank, and when my mom bought us food. I felt terrified, yet secretly proud that Mom had given us this food. But I was also afraid of what my husband would do.

She never spoke of the fake food she had found in my cupboards. Nor did I.

These memories, my mother slipping out the door, the food filling our cupboards, The Husband's angry face, curled around me like smoke, even after the hunger passed.

We eventually had to leave this house and move again to another one.

Note to Readers: If your life is reflecting any of these feelings or events, please seek counseling and trust your inner instincts. Refer to the resources at the back of this book or your city's domestic violence coalition for additional information.

"Love and abuse cannot coexist."

~ bell hooks

Chapter Nine

House of Choking

The Third Son was a stocky baby with hair so fine and blond that it appeared white, and skin so pale and pink that it resembled a blushing rose petal. He smiled all the time as if he felt born into bliss. It didn't matter if the stork mistakenly dropped him off in our home. He saw goodness everywhere and even made me smile.

Third Son was the baby that came after The Husband's failed vasectomy, the doctor's first vasectomy ever, something The Husband never stopped resenting. I had pushed for no more children, but he refused to let me "get fixed," declaring I would become fat and useless. Everyone else tried coaxing him into it, knowing how deeply we lived in poverty with no prospects of improvement that I could see.

I remember us going to the downtown poverty hospital for my usual "female complaints." They called me into an exam room while my husband sat in the waiting room with our two other sons. After some poking and testing, the doctor turned to me with a bright, cheerful face and said, "You're pregnant." He said this with a happy face.

The possibility hadn't even crossed my mind.

Surprised, I burst into tears, which quickly turned into anger.

"How could this be!?" I ranted. "This can't be true! I can't do this again!"

The doctor's expression shifted into concern. "Please don't consider abortion," he said. "I was a baby that was supposed to be aborted but was put up for adoption instead, and I am here helping you!"

Abortion? I had never considered it. In truth, I barely understood much about it.

I ranted and raged and told him, "I couldn't be pregnant. My husband had a vasectomy!"

In an instant, his expression changed, and I saw his suspicions flashing across his face. *Ah, the baby isn't her husband's?*

His demeanor shifted; judgment filled his eyes.

And he stood up and called for security.

I got off the exam table, pulling on my clothes, even though he stood there watching, telling me he would "speak to The Husband." He didn't understand my rage. I flung open the exam room door, which happened to open directly into the large, waiting room filled with patients, my sons, and The Husband.

Framed in the doorway, I yelled as loud as I could with all my rage: "I'M PREGNANT!"

Knowing security was coming, I stalked out past my family and all the gawking faces straight out of the hospital.

I bet those people in the waiting room still retell the story of how this "crazy lady" who screamed about being pregnant, as if it weren't a good thing, a blessing.

The Husband caught up with me, my anger still boiling over. I wasn't afraid of him thinking the baby wasn't his. I knew he was all I had ever been with. But he had never completed the steps for his vasectomy. No retest. No follow-up appointments. Nothing.

He had complained endlessly about the surgery and refused to return to that doctor. Even after I called to tell his office I was pregnant. The doctor had warned us that if we didn't wait a full six months and use protection, pregnancy was possible. He needed to examine The Husband again. (I wondered just what the doctor had snipped.)

But The Husband refused to go back.

The doctor called several times, then finally told me he was leaving the state. The Husband never got rechecked. And he continued to be grieved physically, constantly complaining about the procedure.

I had been raised to believe doctors weren't a viable path to health and that faith held the answers. But faith hadn't saved me yet. And every time I stood in front of a doctor I shrank under their gaze.

Maybe that's why the doctor's judgment hurt me so much. Not just because he suspected me of an illicit love affair, but because he looked at my mental pain and decided it wasn't appropriate. I wasn't allowed to fall apart, nor was I even allowed to have my feelings. My feelings needed security guards.

This pregnancy became an enormous issue. My father-in-law made sly comments about the possibility of "Someone in the woodpile," or "Did my husband really know what I did all day?" while I was present. Even the church people gave me sideways glances, as if they were already sure I had slept with someone else. Judgment was always their first language.

It enraged me. As if I ever could, or *would?*

How would one undertake such an endeavor? I lived in poverty and looked like it, wearing the same second-hand clothes daily, my hair uncut, reflecting the limits of my world. I also had young children, which meant I couldn't even go to the bathroom in private; they followed me everywhere!

What would an adulterous mother do with her babies during such a tryst? Would she shove them in a closet and say, "Don't tell Daddy about the strange man?" It was all so ridiculous and maddening!

I had an ever-curious mind. My oldest had been given a microscope. I used it like a scientist would, sampling my husband's seed (something I certainly had access to). They were wiggling on the slide, proving he could still make babies.

I felt so vindicated! I felt triumphant. So joyful about my "rightness," so sure he would be happy to know too, but he wouldn't even look, wouldn't even get off the sofa to see. He acted like my attempt at science was disgusting.

Perhaps it was . . . Looking back, it wasn't just about the wiggling evidence on the slide. It was about truth, visible, undeniable truth, and how it was still dismissed the moment it came from me.

That moment branded something deep inside me. It wasn't about facts. It was about who got to tell the story, and I was never allowed to be the storyteller.

I went to church less and less, keeping even more to myself. No one cared about the truth or even the issue of what to do now, since he was *still fertile.*

Especially not my husband.

Shouldn't he do something?

He asked me to bring him another beer.

As my belly grew with the child the stork had dropped on our doorstep, my anger and sadness simmered beneath everything I did. Of course, I loved my babies. I would stare into their tiny faces, promising them a better life, a good life, if only my love could make that happen.

I no longer believed that a good life was waiting for us.

My heart had long since broken.

With my third son's arrival, the hospital sent a small squeeze tube of medicine to put into my new baby's eyes, daily until his next checkup. They said it was to prevent diseases from getting a foothold in his eyes from birth, specifically, STDs. I remember feeling insulted. How could I have gotten anything like that? I rarely left the house. The idea of dealing with anyone else in bed, when I could barely tolerate what was required by marriage, was absurd.

I saw birth as a natural process that the body handled quite well, but mothering had so many challenging moments. Still, I dutifully held my baby down, pried open his bright blue eye with the fingers of one hand, and applied the cream from the tube with the other. He fussed and squirmed every time.

Who wouldn't?

One night, his fussing erupted into full-throated screams. He knew exactly what was coming. His tiny arms flailed, his whole body stiff with protest. So much more than usual. I cajoled him quietly, soothingly, mindful of The Husband out in the living room going about his nightly job of drinking himself unconscious.

But this baby was not having any of it. His strength was amazing as he pushed his stocky arms against my efforts, his screams intensifying. It seemed impossible to manage him.

Suddenly, The Husband lurched into the room and shoved me aside. He swayed by the bed, glaring at me through drunken, bloodshot eyes.

"What are you doing?" He slurred, as if He hadn't seen me doing it since the baby was born. He reeked of alcohol.

"Trying to put the medicine in his eyes," I whispered, dread crawling up my spine.

He demanded that I give him the cream tube. Fear prickled the back of my neck as He snatched it from my fingers.

He staggered and dropped down over our son, who was now full-on wailing. The baby had squeezed his eyes tightly shut; his whole skin turned a deep, purplish red. With thick, clumsy fingers, The Husband tried inexpertly to force the baby's eyelids open, gouging, sliding, and poking at him with the ointment tube.[1]

A hot, violent rage shot through me, a kind of wild heat I didn't know I was capable of. I lunged at the husband, clawing, pulling, trying to wrench him from our baby. I attempted to grab my son from the bed.

With shocking speed, I didn't think The drunk Husband was capable of, he backhanded me away, launching us both up against the bedroom wall. His hands around my neck.[2] He lifted me slightly from the floor as he tightened his grip around my throat, then squeezed tighter and tighter.

I was a little taller than he was, but his drunken strength and stocky build were shocking and powerful. I couldn't breathe and found myself stunned. His face swam and warped as I stared at him. Red, furious words drenched in alcohol, spit out at me.

"Don't you EVER try to keep me from my son! I know what I am doing!"

His drunken breath hot on my face, wild eyes glaring into mine. I froze with fear, feet dangling, my hands gripping his wrists, unable to think clearly.

Then, as suddenly as he had thrown me against the wall, he dropped me.

He staggered out of the room without another word.

Our son had grown strangely quiet.

I crawled onto the bed, gathered him to me, and curled around him, rocking us both with small sobs, my throat aching.

At that moment, something inside me cracked open, a truth I didn't have words for yet.

I wanted to believe our love would be different. Not full of fear. That people who said they loved you didn't hurt you like that. It had never once crossed my mind to harm anyone, let alone someone I loved so purposely, so how could he say he loved us? That thought swirled in my chest like smoke, bitter and inescapable.

I knew something was deeply wrong. I would need to find the strength to sort this out, to find a way to heal our marriage. But strength was not what I felt; it was just solid fear.

Fear of Him.

Fear for my babies.

And the terrible knowledge that I had nowhere to go and no one to talk to about this shameful event, or even about our whole life.

He never mentioned what had happened between us afterward.

(Did he even remember what he had done?)

I could not speak of it.

My fear wrapped itself around my throat the way his hands had.

Thereafter, my hand occasionally traveled to my neck as if wondering if it *really* happened, but the bruises told no lies. I could not pretend that it hadn't happened, even if he could.

Sometimes, even today, as an old woman, my hand drifts to my neck. The bruises have been gone for decades, but the memory remains.

Maybe I just wasn't submissive enough. Perhaps I wasn't grateful enough. The church continued to insist that women were required to submit to their husbands' leadership in all things. They preached it as holiness, the divine order of the family. I'd sit in church looking over all the families and wonder:

How many wives had been choked?

How many were raped, on the regular?

How many are left to live on white rice for days?[2, 3]

If I had understood the underpinnings of marriage, I would have chosen anything else.

Anything.

But my lack of maturity, the need to leave my family home, not knowing myself, and just the pathetic gratitude that someone had professed to love me, had all delivered me into this life.

After the choking, Something in my spirit shifted. Not instantly, not cleanly, more like a hairline fracture that kept widening each time life pressed down.

I still had no words for what I was living in. But I had learned the rules of my world well:

He was the head of the household.

His anger was my burden.

My silence was my safety.

Life moved forward in the slow, stunning way that trauma does. Nothing discussed, nothing acknowledged, nothing healed. He went on drinking. I went on mothering.

The danger of saying anything to anyone felt immense. Who would believe me? Who would I tell? My church taught that suffering was a holy experience, sometimes brought about by your own sins. My family taught me marriage was final. And my husband taught me that speaking up meant punishment.

So, I moved more quietly through the house, shrinking my world smaller and smaller. I became hyper-aware of every sound he made, the scrape of his shoes on the carpet, the sigh before he opened his beer, the pitch of his voice when something had already set him off. My body lived in readiness, scanning every shift of his posture, every flicker in his eyes, trying to protect against the next danger.

The Ponderings

Love. What a strange word for what we lived. Somewhere deep inside, a small voice began whispering: *This is not love, not normal,* and once it started, it never stopped.

I was beginning to understand that love didn't mean the same thing to everyone. Each person defined it differently, and some definitions could hurt. The Husband's definition of love was simple: *"The more I did for him, supposedly equated to how much I loved him."* But no matter how much I did, it was never enough. I didn't know my love language.

I tried to believe what I learned in church, that love meant showing overt concern and care for one another. That someone would demonstrate it by caring for you and your feelings. I don't even think I had a clear idea of what love really was, but I knew the love I wanted to believe in didn't exist in my marriage, and I was sure of it.

By this time, I had learned that I had no rights and no needs more important than The Husband's.[4] I did everything required of me methodically, quietly, and carefully so that he would have no complaints. I had grown accustomed to his gaslighting—telling me things and then denying he ever said them, insisting I had caused him to punch a hole in the wall by bringing home the wrong salad dressing, and so much more.[5]

My life's constraints wrapped around me, chafing my skin raw, and breaking my heart daily. When he wasn't home, I felt more alive, as if I were becoming two people instead of one.

The boys and I played and rallied in what ways we could, always making sure we cleaned up and had everything in order before he returned home.

Once, we were shrieking and laughing and dancing in a rain-filled backyard mud puddle, all of us covered in brown, slick mud and delight, when the mailman's head suddenly appeared over the back gate, his eyes wide with wonder. We froze, dripping, staring back at him.

"Was just wondering if 'en you-all was okay?" he said, shaking his head, adding, "White people is shore crazy!"

We laughed even harder, laughing until our tears blended into the mud.

When The Husband was away, it was as if a breath had been released. The boys and I played with abandon, dragging sheets over the furniture to build hideaway forts, and making up games. I played right alongside them, not just as their mother but as someone rediscovering the joy of being alive.

It was the only time I felt like me. That *girl*, the one with imagination and wonder, who had always been there, never allowed to grow up all the way. I think *she* might have been fun if *she'd* been given the chance. Every time the door closed behind The Husband, as he left for work, we shed fear, like stuffy church clothes, and ran towards joy.

Much later, in another house, in another life, I found an old cane and dressed up in my heeled church shoes and a coat of tails I had made. Dancing across the foyer just like the women on TV did, with their high kicks and swaggers, I hummed a light-hearted and bold tune. The Husband turned from his TV, staring at me, his face showing disgust, and asked what the hell I thought I was doing. I stopped, under his withering stare, and quietly folded up that piece of myself and tucked her away. Hiding her away all those years had a cost too high to measure. You can't even calculate the loss in human terms, all those joyful moments missed, not learning to be the real me.

By then, I had three babies, and we were not living the life I had dreamed for them or me. Nobody was helping me, and nobody was going to save us from our foolishness. So, I thought I could. It wasn't wisdom, not yet. It was initially rebellion, then survival. The world around me had made it clear that if I wanted my children to have even the slightest chance at something better, I'd have to become the one to make it happen.

I had managed to sneak away one day. Doing so was always a fearful event, as I did not want to get caught leaving the children with the neighbor, which was a monumental sin according to The Husband.[6] My job was to stick to my role. I wanted to walk to Planned Parenthood to try to get fixed so no more babies would come into this home.[7] I had begged the birth doctor to fix me at 3rd Son's birth, but he had patted me and said I was much too young for such a decision.

I grimaced at his words. He had no idea how much I had aged inside in grief, or how I lived.

My heart knew so much better than that doctor that having more babies was NOT a good idea. Our house needed a large "No Storks Here" sign on its roof, painted in bright red. Planned Parenthood provided me with the necessary paperwork to complete, which I filled out laboriously. However, they informed me that The Husband would need to sign his approval when I returned it to the desk.

I seriously raged all the way home, my shoes slapping the sidewalk to the beat of my anger, the unfairness of being a woman, at my life, at everything, curling God's ears with my words. The Husband would never sign it, and of course, it never occurred to me to lie and say I wasn't married or fake his signature.

How could I ever have hidden such an event, even if I had managed it? It was all so absurd. This happened long before a cell phone in your hand could educate you on almost anything, and before I could bring the world into my own home through a computer. Slowly, though, I began to uncover the truth about how we lived and the wrongness of it.

I despised myself for doing whatever I could to avoid raising The Husband's anger. I became skilled at pretending life was just dandy, avoiding desires, and keeping my hopes low to avoid disappointment. Pretending meant wearing a smile even when I felt hollow inside. It meant answering "I'm fine" when I hadn't felt fine in years. It meant swallowing my thoughts before they reached my lips, keeping my shoulders from slumping, and never asking for anything, not even small comforts.

I pretended to be content, not because I genuinely felt it, but because I had learned from an early age that acting like everything was fine was what good little girls, good daughters, and good wives were supposed to do. Sadly, unrealized by me, even my boys began to believe in the show, their little eyes watching me for cues on how to be okay when things were not. I became the actress in a play that no one applauded, yet everyone still expected me to perform.

Did The Husband do things with us? I can count on one hand the few times he had in all the years we were together. We remember the disappointments far more; isn't that how life is? Sometimes, he promised to take us to the park, or a church function, but he seldom did. We knew nothing good would happen once he returned from the market with a bottle.

I had started to stop believing in him long before, but I still tried to keep the spark alive for the sake of my sons. I thought maybe if I just believed hard enough for all of us, I could buy them a little more time to be boys. Time to hope, time to not know the truth about our family. When he failed us again, choosing the bottle over the park, I scrambled to patch the day together with my own hands. But eventually, I couldn't protect The Husband from himself, and I couldn't protect our boys from their quiet heartbreak either.

A child's disappointment leaves no bruise, but it echoes in their heart far into the future. I didn't know it then, but a child neglected by their father won't know how to become an engaged father themselves without help.

The Husband went away one weekend on a hiking campout with his guy friends, which I foolishly thought I could join. (Didn't I go hiking and camping with my family?) He laughed at me and said with total authority, "Babies and mothers don't go camping." But I knew that wasn't true. Before marriage, I had seen fathers hiking with babies on their backs and mothers walking with them in the Desolation Wilderness.

My whole life had been condensed down to the walls of this small home, with its tiny backyard and way too many useless plum trees. I couldn't grow food in the soil there due to too much shade and gnarled roots. Those trees dropped yellow nickel-sized sour plums in season, primarily useless for eating. The tall tree out front had heart-shaped persimmons that were terribly bitter, and when ripe, they splattered onto the tiny, cracked driveway, lost to my lack of knowledge on how to use them.

My days were filled with all the chores the church had deemed a good wife should do, along with the endless care of now three babies, raising them in the ways of the church. There was never any time for me, and the *me* that might have bloomed began to disappear. Worse than The Husband's hands around my neck, the house felt like it was choking the life out of me. Every chore was suffocating.

Ultimately, feral thoughts began crossing my mind day by day. More than anything, I just wanted to run away from it all and never look back. Surely this couldn't be what all life was all about?

I wouldn't have known if you had asked me what I liked, what I wanted to do, or what my favorite anything was. It didn't matter anyway, as all that mattered was what The Husband wanted. I knew the taste of sadness and despair, and knew I couldn't do this forever.

Even though I wanted to run, something strange had happened to me over the years, and I had become afraid to leave my home. The very houses that trapped me also became the only world I knew. The longer I stayed, the harder it was to go. I wasn't just bound by his control, but by my own fear of the outside world. The unknown felt more dangerous than the hell I already knew.

Looking back, I see now how captivity reprograms the mind, how fear wraps itself around your choices until freedom itself starts to look like a threat. It wasn't just the lock on the gate that kept me inside or the closed doors. It was the ones forming inside me.

Perhaps more than one fundamental flaw in me prevented me from creating the perfect home with a smiling, happy husband and children. Maybe it was the wrong kind of hope that kept me trying: a desperate hope, a hollow hope. The kind that whispers, "Try harder, be better, stay one more day," even when the truth is choking you.

All the things the church taught didn't seem to help, nor did my fervently ardent prayers. I became obsessed with the thought that everything would magically fall into place if I could find the right recipe for life and "the proper" knowledge.

There came a time when The Husband had a preemptive talk *at* me. The circumstances surrounding why he gave me the "talk" have blown away in the years since it occurred, but not the words, repeated in different forms throughout later years. Their meaning has stuck like an old, rusted jar lid. He said, *"If you try to take the kids away, you'll never get them. I'll see to it. I'll tell everyone you're a horrible mother. I'll tell them stuff, so you'll never even be allowed to see them."* [8]

These words were always said in perfect calm and with a steely knowing in his eyes, during his alcohol stupor, as he wasn't given to talking while sober. Of course, I believed him. My heart had stuttered the first time he said it. Perhaps he could hear my feral thoughts.

There was nothing to tattle about that I could imagine. If I could have fully embraced perfection, perhaps our lives would have been better. I had immersed myself in being a church lady and homemaker, taking it seriously as my job. But there were those thoughts…

I would look away when he said such things, without a rebuttal, lest he could read my mind. "Just run away, run away," I would be thinking. Perfect wives don't think about running away.

But one of his old church friends' wives had done it. She had as many children as I did, yet she disappeared and left them. She was *roasted* by the church gossipers, of course. They pecked her apart like a flock of chickens on a dropped apple.

In my mind, I understood. I applauded her bravery, feeling both frightened and envious. She was unable to have her children after leaving. Sometimes, I thought her husband had been even worse than mine. How hard it must have been for her to leave her children behind, *but I understood.*

I knew The Husband couldn't "tell" anyone that I had snuck away to find food, or even that I had left the babies with the neighbor lady. Those things were only sins to him. It would make him appear not to be providing for his family. There was nothing to tattle on except for my dark thoughts.

I explored those deeply buried thoughts in the dark of the night, exhuming them with the sounds of my sleeping family and the creaks and groans of the old house whispering in my ears. Could I ever even do such a thing? Run away? And where would I go? Could I take all these babies and really keep them? Could I even leave them behind? Could my heart stand that?

I feared my own mind. Those thoughts, those wild thoughts, felt like intrusions from Satan himself. That's what I had been taught, after all. I wasn't acting on them but thinking about them was almost as bad. Guilt clung to me like a second skin, even though they were just cries for help from a heart that could take no more.

I had thought The Husband's family was influential. His dad was a deacon in the church. He had a significant presence and ruled his family from the top down, as the church instructed. I did, however, have some insight into how his wife felt and what she had endured. She had become my closest friend and confidant. There were others in the church I considered friends. I may not have shared my life with them, for self-preservation, but all of these people were meaningful to me. I would be giving up all I had ever known, everyone I had grown up with, if I decided to leave.

I must have dreamed up so many scenarios and ideas that came to nothing. I felt too ashamed and more afraid of the unknown possibilities *out in the world*, than of the things that I lived with every day.

The whole world was an unknown possibility.

One morning, after much deliberation, I made a conscious, firm decision to stay.

Just stay. Stop thinking of leaving.

Just stay. Tasting the bitterness of the words. I said it out loud to myself while looking down at my son, *"I'm making a choice to stay."* It wasn't surrender. It was something else. I had no map, no rescue, and no room to run, but still, I chose. It wasn't that I didn't want to run. I didn't know *where* to run that wouldn't hurt my children more.

The world had taught me that a mother stays. The church praised women who endured. Everywhere I turned, the message was the same: stay, sacrifice, serve. So, I stayed. Not because it was *right*, but because I saw no safe way to leave. And because I believed I was the only shield my children had. That choice, quiet as it was, marked the beginning of a life I would have to forge myself. I had no words for it then, only a mother's fierce love and a woman's buried grit.

I needed to make this conscious decision, to give up thoughts of getting away, of escaping to any other better life. This was the life I had. With no money, no safe harbor elsewhere, and without the ability to drive, this was my life. The tension of trying to hold both thoughts of my duty and the deep desire to escape had become overwhelming.

I tried to dismiss the thought of running away despite my circumstances. I looked at my sleeping second son's sweet face as I passed by, knowing all that stood between him and this crazy world was me. He wasn't like my first son or my new third son. My mother's heart sensed this. If the Internet had existed then, it would have said "possible autism." Later, testing revealed he was on the autism spectrum and had hearing loss, as well as other birth defects.

My pregnancy lacked the best nutrition, and his birth had been long and hard. I could never desert him and his brothers to a drunken father. No one believed me when I said there was something different about this baby, but I knew. I knew it in the way he flinched when held, pulling away from me. The way his eyes couldn't quite meet mine, the way sound and language didn't seem to find him. I didn't have the right words back then. There was no easy diagnosis, no helpful teacher, and no specialist doctors. There was just me, doing my best to love a child who didn't respond like my first baby. Still, I loved him fiercely, even when that love looked like sitting in silence beside him under the table, where he spent a lot of time sheltering himself from the world.

The Danger of Knowledge

I wanted to become a better mom, to be the best person I could be, but I needed more help. One day, I escaped to the library, about six blocks away, and discovered self-help books. I also found books on alcoholism, codependency, and abuse tucked onto shelves (not near the Christian parenting and marriage titles). I had, however, discovered that knowledge came with strong emotions and pain, and that knowing carried a heavy price. I couldn't "unknow" the things I had learned. The truth about how we were living. The truth about The Husband's alcoholism, abuse, and my codependency.

The bitterness felt and tasted worse than powdered alum on the tongue.

All we were, at that moment, were statistics, sad, sorry statistics, certainly NOT chosen ones.

I thought that learning the truth would set me free, but it only made the walls feel closer.

The books didn't tell me how to escape. They told me how to endure. On every page, I saw proof that our suffering wasn't rare. It was common. We weren't some cursed exceptions in this life. We were textbook, predictable, a case study. After all the prayers and obedience, all the sacrifices and second chances, after years of believing we were chosen, *we were just a statistic!*

That truth filled me with hot, wild anger, not just at myself and The Husband but at the whole system that kept women like me locked in place, handing us coping skills instead of keys.

This world doesn't feel like it was designed for women to have personal freedom. Even when we do get a glimpse of it, we're not taught how to carry it. We are taught how to carry children, carry shame, and carry silence, but not freedom. That's a whole different weight altogether, and without guidance, it can feel heavier than the chains we are trying to escape.

I read the books while he was away. I read them late at night when he passed out, and I read all I could find. It didn't make me better. It didn't encourage me. I felt overwhelmingly buried and sad. Cheated. Lied to. By my God. By myself. By our families.

By the realization that my mother's prophecy—*"He will become a fat drunk who is mean to you"*—was coming true right before my eyes.

And by my husband, who had taken alcohol to bed like a mistress and worked hard to fulfill that prophecy, leaving me alone in the wreckage of our life.

Most of all, I stood in a bone-deep sadness at *myself*, for the life I had helped create and could no longer deny.

I knew then the "wrongness" of it all. Our entire lives had been a farce, just like my parents', a reality fabricated and lived outside of any genuine understanding. Whatever The Husband deemed to be the truth, he expected me to believe it as gospel. Whatever the church decreed right and proper, I was supposed to accept as gospel. I felt anger rising...so much anger.

Knowledge had birthed an unbeliever. I began to distrust everything and rethink what I had learned in my life. The church warned of such thinking. Satan roamed the earth looking for those who would fall away from belief because they had re-tasted the tree of the knowledge of good and evil. I could practically feel Satan's breath tickling the hairs on the back of my neck as I read.

The library books had flung open the folds of my mind, shining a bright light into its dusty corners. The knowledge piling up in my mind tugged and pushed against the knowing of my whole life, and my relationship with the God of my fathers. My mind roiled with conflict. The knowledge struggled to sit side-by-side with what I lived: my beliefs that didn't align with reality; duties that had become shackles; and love that never quite resembled love.

Sometimes I looked at The Husband's peaceful face as he slept and mourned the loss of the love I had felt for him in the beginning, feeling confused, weary, and hopeless. His dark lashes lay on his cheeks with the innocence of how he must have been as a child. Days flitted through my mind as though I sat in a time machine, watching all the way back to our beginning. Where had we gone wrong? Where was the secret that would fix everything? Why had I said "yes" that day? What a naïve little fool I had been.

It wasn't long before that misdirected stork found our home again, and soon I would have my Fourth son, born into the worst dysfunction we had yet to live through. *Again, what had that doctor snipped?*

At the same time, slowly, a change occurred inside me, a shift from a tender heart to a sturdiness I had never experienced before. Believing in something on my own seemed more complicated and far more difficult than sitting among the many church people I knew, all believing together. These were the people I had grown up with year after year. Our lives together had meaning. There was sweetness and pain.

The Husband continued to remind me that "I never did anything right, I wasn't good enough, was ungrateful and unlovable, and I would never find anyone else who would love me."

To trust myself, I had to leap over all that and discover a different truth, which I chose to make my own. I was beginning to strike out into the world, with only myself to hold my hand.

If I couldn't move the elephants in the room, I'd have to find a way around them.

We eventually had to leave this house and move again to another one.

Note to Readers: If your life is reflecting any of these feelings or events, please seek counseling and trust your inner instincts. Refer to the resources at the back of this book or your city's domestic violence coalition for additional information.

The Inheritance

When my mother passed her inheritance to me, she couldn't have known it would become seed money in the most literal sense. That gift became rows of beans, corn, and squash, food I could put on the table, so my family would never go hungry again. It was more than money. It was a promise that survival could grow from the ground beneath our feet.

All the knowledge my mother passed down about growing food became the real inheritance, something I could offer my children and use to change our lives.

The new house we moved to became the best place for our bellies. It came with a huge, fenced yard. I stood on the useless scrub grass and imagined tearing up half of it to plant food and watering the other half to create a lawn for kids to play on.

Back when I was young, I groaned and sweated through long summer days helping my mother garden. She would drive from plot to plot, planting, weeding, and picking. We had plenty then, and I didn't yet know hunger was possible. After the harvest, we canned, froze, and delivered extras to people in need. I sat on a stool beside the pressure cooker, listening to it chit-chit-chit like a metal beast on the stove. I watched the pressure dial carefully, sweat pouring down my neck, adjusting the gas flame to keep it steady. My mom had frightened me with well-meaning stories about how pressure cookers were prone to blowing up if not handled correctly, so my eyes never strayed far from the dial. I hated it. My brothers didn't have to help. All I wanted to do was run free, climb trees, and explore the neighborhood. I used to feel used and abused as the only girl in the home. I never realized she was handing me the skill that would one day save us.

We had moved to one of the poorest places yet, where the Bloods and Crips gangs controlled opposing boundaries. A drug and weapons dealer lived on one side of our home, and on the other, a woman who might have been just as trapped as I was.

Here at this new house, I swallowed my pride and asked my mother for garden help. She had kept the lawn and garden business we had started years earlier. She brought her rototiller, tools, and supplies, including seeds, mulch, fertilizer, and everything I needed to get started. She must have been remembering the time she saw my bare cupboards.

I didn't care how hard it might be. There would be no more hunger in this House. It took just one season of hard tending to create a stunning garden. The fencing around our yard was see-through wire, with barbed wire at the top, which put my work on display to the whole neighborhood. A large gate opened to the back, and that was how my mom got her truck in and out whenever she dropped off supplies or leaves that I could compost. My mother never stayed long, just dropped off what she had and left. There was never much conversation. I didn't know how to welcome her with The Husband there. He tolerated her visits but the tension was thick and oppressive.

Still, nearly every day neighbors paused to gawk, as if I had planted a herd of Unicorns instead of a garden. In our poverty-stricken neighborhood, yards held old sofas, broken-down junk cars, and trash. There was very little beauty. With my mother's knowledge, the soil bloomed beneath my hands, and since I stayed home to care for the family, the garden became an extension of that care. Weeds barely had a chance. Every plant seemed to pose for the Johnny's Seed Catalog. Sunflowers stretched 12 feet tall, their platter-sized heads turning with the light. Long, purple Thai beans curled inches from their trellis. I grew herbs, potatoes, squash, tomatoes, onions, garlic, and spices. Nearly everything needed to make a good meal.

One day, I found a Vietnamese family standing patiently at the back gate. They stared at the garden with quiet reverence. With my hands and expressions, I asked them if they would like to come in. The parents herded their children in, and they all stepped softly through the rows, their fingers gently brushing the leaves. No one spoke. They dipped their heads in a gesture of thanks as I offered them food that was ready to harvest. Maybe they had once known gardens like this in their homeland. The neighborhood called them "boat people," a slur that didn't account for their humanity. Forced to live in cramped apartments with tiny yards, they couldn't grow what they once had. I understood that a bit, underneath the surprise of my own life. I hadn't known what I was getting into either.

In those years, we only went to the store for what we couldn't grow. My children didn't have access to many processed foods. Snacks, sodas, and packaged treats were extreme luxuries we couldn't afford. Instead, their plates overflowed with steamed potatoes, carrots, beans, parsnips, and so much more.

My mother often brought me plants that others no longer wanted. Our entire yard soon bloomed with the flowers and plants we adopted. I wanted food, and we needed it, but I also craved beauty. The many colorful wildflowers in our yard gave me joy. They drew the bees, which helped the plants, which fed us, all through the work of my dirt-covered hands and my mother's gifted knowledge.

When the growing season was over and everything was put to rest for the winter, my mother brought over more bags full of leaves that she had raked up from other jobs and piled them high over the garden. I tried to teach my boys how to grow plants, show them how they could feed themselves, and give them the same connection I had learned from my mother. I slowly worked at turning all those leaves under into the dirt. And by spring, there was rich, loamy, dark soil ready to grow again.

As long as the garden produced food, we had enough to eat. But I had no way to preserve it. Canning jars and a pressure cooker were luxuries I couldn't afford for years. Still, that first garden changed everything. It reminded me that no matter where we landed, I could bring life from the ground. I could make beauty in the midst of brokenness. It was my secret happiness. It was a place that looked like work but actually filled my soul with meaning and delight.

I tried to instill in my sons, in little ways, the importance of growing food. We were poor, but we didn't have to eat food from the food bank or junk food from the gas stations. I could fill my sons' plates with steamed vegetables and homegrown potatoes, and know I was giving them good food. I hoped some of this would stick with them through their lives. I did not know it then, but we weren't just surviving. I was planting something that would last far into the future, passing on a food heritage my mother had given me.

Chapter Ten

House of Turning Wheels

Permission to Work and Its Burdens

Far in the future, when money became scarcer and The Husband's need for drink grew, he begrudgingly allowed me to earn an income, as long as it didn't interfere with my other responsibilities and chores. And most importantly, I was told to use the money for bills.[1]

Being allowed to work felt like a tremendous freedom, but it came wrapped in chains. I was desperate for the chance to earn my own money. I believed it would change everything. But it also meant doing it on top of everything else I was already required to deal with: the chores, the children, a house that had to be ready for Jesus at all times, the yard work, garden, and a Husband who offered little help. I began to resent his rule even more. Church left a bitterness in my mouth. I resented it and the systems that told me I was created to serve endlessly, but not to speak or have a say in my own life.

Some days, even being a woman was too difficult. It felt like every institution, church, marriage, and tradition needed to keep its collective boot on a woman's neck to keep itself standing. At first, I truly believed the doctrine that I was responsible for keeping the house holy, the children obedient, and the table set for Christ's return. But the more I lived it, the more I saw the lie in it. The weight was always on the woman. We made the meals, bore the children, did the teaching, cleaned the house, and softened the edges of life, yet still, we were treated less than.

The fact that I would have to go out and work for money and then come home and do all the same homemaker chores, often late into the night, did not matter. Yes, it didn't seem fair that a man could come home from his job, drink himself to sleep, and do *literally* nothing else because of his privilege of being born a man. But deep inside, I knew I was the one who had made this *"bed to lie in,"* and I believed I had little right to complain.

Using My Talent

I had answered an ad in the newspaper for "Artists Needed." I didn't actually consider myself an artist, but I had talent, and maybe this was something I could do. The thought of earning my own money was so tantalizing that it overcame my fears of being out in public, of going somewhere new and far, and of not being good enough. I didn't give myself a moment to think. I set aside all my fears and went to the interview.

When we pulled up to their shop, a line of people stretched outside, each holding a professional artist's portfolio and dressed in fine clothes. I felt my first stab of fear and a sense of lack. I wore what I had, and my artwork was in a black plastic garbage bag, the only container I had to use for my paintings. I stood in the line with my head down, my face red from the humiliation, clearly seeing that I might not fit in. Determination kept my feet in the line. I didn't speak to anyone, but I felt their eyes on me, clutching my black plastic garbage bag with sweaty hands.

Once in the room with the shop owners, they described to me what the job entailed: painting designs by famous artists on needlework canvases for people to purchase and work yarn into. They asked me several questions about how long and where I had received my art schooling, at which point I had to admit I had none. Their faces told me it wasn't what they wanted to hear, and I knew my desperation showed. Before they could dismiss me, I asked if I could show them my work, which I pulled out of the garbage bag, feeling foolish as it crinkled. My artwork was strong, and I saw their reaction. They looked especially impressed when they asked how long it had taken to finish each painting and heard how quickly it had been completed. They asked me an important question, judging by the looks on their faces. "What would you do if you accidentally painted outside the lines onto the tan-colored canvas?"

These were to be needlework projects representing famous artists from the past and required exact copies. I pondered the question carefully, and because my past has always been filled with "necessity being the mother of invention," I said I would mix up a color exactly to match the background and paint over my mistake.

They looked at each other with apparent delight and wonder, then turned back to me and exclaimed in unison, "Why didn't we think of that!" And I got the job!

In my heart, this work represented more than just a job. It lit up a pathway to freedom. I had done this on my own, something that might allow me to meet my own needs and, maybe one day, provide my children and me with a new life. My life experiences had taught me to wait for the other shoe to drop, as it always seemed to do. Then, the truth of life would manifest itself in that dropped shoe lying on the dusty floor, proving that disappointment and bitterness were never far behind.

The thought of money trickling in softened the Husband's stance, and he grudgingly agreed to help. However, soon the reality of driving back and forth and watching the children for a few hours each week quickly drained his enthusiasm. I was much slower at painting these precious canvases because acrylics were new to me, and the fear that I wouldn't be good enough rippled through my brush strokes. Others had also been hired, and we all sat in a large workroom painting. I don't remember what I earned for each canvas. It wasn't much, but I knew I'd have to paint faster to be valuable.

At work, I sat in a room with other women "of the world," painting and listening to their confident chatter, and all it did was remind me how much I didn't belong there.

It was my first experience being an adult out in the world, aside from attending school. I stayed quiet, my secret, shameful family life hidden away from any conversation. I just listened and painted, saying very little. As in all my school years, people tended to group, with me being the odd one out, just as I was here. The absolute thrill of being out and using my skills was more than enough joy.

The Husband finally said I would have to quit, as it wasn't worth the effort he had to put in for the money it brought in.[2] My grief felt so devastating. The slight taste of freedom and use of my talents had made me dream and hope again. It would have been better never to have tried. I cried long and hard because the "other shoe had dropped."

When I went in there to tell them I couldn't work for them anymore, everything in me burned with shame and anger. They surprised me by saying I could take my canvases home, work on them, and return them when finished! They didn't offer this to the others, but they loved my work. For the first time in my married life, something good had happened, and I'd inspired it myself. Unbelievably, they thought my work had value! There wasn't much income, and most of it went to bills, but here and there, I earned a few dollars to hold on to.

It began changing me. It wasn't like when the cartoon character Popeye ate spinach, making his muscles instantly pop out on his arms so he could take on the world's challenges. It wasn't like that. Instead, it happened slowly and steadily. I felt a specific power and strength that my mind hadn't had before. Maybe all the bad things I had been told about myself weren't entirely true.

Eventually, the company let us all go as their idea did not increase sales, as they had hoped. When the owner had the severance talk with me, she told me that I was such a good artist and that I should be out there painting and selling my art. That phrase danced in my heart and mind, echoing on my bad days with the potential of possibility.

The Feel of Two Thousand Dollars

I found it hard to imagine, impossible even, that my grandma had left me $2,000 when she passed. My grandma, whom I rarely saw, knew next to nothing about me. She thought of me before she died. I never had so much money and marveled over Grandma's gift. She died a poor woman. How did she do it? But I was worried. I worried that The Husband would learn of the money and declare it for himself.[3]

Guilt rose as I knew I'd have to keep it a secret as long as possible.

What I needed was to buy a car of my own. A vehicle would change things for me, I was sure of it! My sister-in-law sold me her old yellow Pontiac, which was big enough to hold my family. Honestly, I don't remember how the car ended up in our driveway or how the money was exchanged. It was a monumental moment, representing the freedom it could afford.

After coming from work, the Husband spied it and demanded to know where it had come from. I told him I had bought it from his sister, with money from my deceased grandma.

Buying it from his sister was indeed a point in my favor. But he was not happy, not at all. My whole body tightened as I worried about what he would do next.

He had taken up smoking, so he smoked and stared silently at the car while pacing around it. Eventually, he squatted down and, in silence, let the air out of every tire until my car sat wilted in the driveway. I knew better than to protest. He walked past me, flicking the cigarette butt aside, and said, "When you can fix the tires, you can drive it."[4]

Later, I picked up the butt and put it in the trash.

His cruelty was a stab in my heart. Four flat tires were not an easy fix for me, and I still needed to renew my old driver's license. The Husband had always refused to let me, saying he'd drive me anywhere I needed to go, and my having a car wasn't necessary.[5]

I would jump through these hurdles with determination to have freedom.

My first son had made "friends" with another boy in the neighborhood. The boy's Uncle, with The Husband's permission, gave them both regular rides to their new school. One day, the man noticed my new car, squatting on flat tires in our driveway, and asked if I needed help.

(I felt sure First Son had probably told him the whole story.) It went against The Husband's (and perhaps the church's) rules to have another man on the property when he was not there, and I grew very nervous, as he could come home at any time. This Uncle could be both helpful and a potential danger. I told him it was very kind of him but not to worry. I would handle the problem.

He was a rather intimidating character, standing over six feet tall and muscular. He wore many tatts on his arms and face, and a biking jacket from some club; a veteran who was haunted by scars that weren't visible. He had a way of trying to be genuinely kind and cautious around me, and he seemed aware that his very size and look might scare off some people. His family assured me that he would not harm the boys and that it would be safe for us to allow him to drive them both the few blocks to their school.

Despite my earlier protests, the Uncle returned the very next day with an air compressor and began filling the car tires. I should have known fate would twist the moment, as The Husband came home before he finished. I felt embarrassed and humiliated when The Husband scolded me in front of the person who had tried to help. Maybe he felt intimidated by the Uncle, as he stood much shorter and softer now, no match against the other man in any way. The Uncle held his hands up as if to ward off my husband and said he'd leave. The Husband kept trying to escalate the altercation, yammering at the fellow. I could hear the Uncle say, "Just trying to help a neighbor!" as he retrieved his equipment.

Yes, I paid for that incident, even though I had told the Uncle I didn't need help and had tried to discourage him. To make matters worse, the Uncle came over the next day without permission, filled the other two tires, and left. He saluted me from the end of the driveway.

Perhaps my husband figured that letting all the air out again would result in more unwanted visitors, so he left the car alone. In time, the car became my wings. But for now, it could not fly me far enough away, as I always had to return home.

The Shift of Power

The Husband drank more and more after we moved to this rundown area full of deeper poverty and despair. It felt like one of the most challenging places we had ever lived. This home sat in a ramshackle neighborhood, wedged between newer homes and the hum of the freeway. Neighbors were given over to the indignity of poverty, often sitting on their porches staring out into the middle distance, smoking and idle, like they were waiting for something to happen, anything that might break up their day.

Then came the car accident between my husband and another driver. It was the other driver's fault, but the drinking had already taken its toll on his mind. Afterward, he quit work and withdrew into the home, brooding and spending the three-thousand-dollar settlement on alcohol. When that money ran out and rent loomed unpaid, fear of homelessness drove me to call my mom, asking for just enough to cover it. Our calls were rare. I had never asked for money before, and I felt awful asking. She turned me down with a laugh. Desperate, I took my African grey parrot, a gift from my father, to a pet store and sold him to pay for the rent. I was heartbroken and angry at the man slumped in a stupor on the sofa.

If I'd ever felt love for him, it was dissolving fast.

The following month, The Husband sold his handgun to pay the rent, something I was relieved to see go. Still, he blamed me for our decline as if I had brought this upon us. Conversations I'd never imagined were now commonplace. He drank and brooded, and I began crossing lines that church teachings said I should not.

Our marriage fractured under the weight of survival. In this fracture, I began to find my courage, standing up to his control. I told him he could no longer take the kids with him when he went out to buy his bottles, or wherever he went. With him being drunk, it wasn't safe, *and he was always drunk.* Saying that out loud was nearly unthinkable to me, and infuriating to him, but even he couldn't dispute the truth.

I began paying more attention to the bills and how we would cover them. And I refused to be intimate with him when he was drinking. *Each step I took chipped away at his authority, but it also chipped away at my fear, teaching me that survival sometimes meant breaking the rules I had been taught to obey.*

As we continued to stress over food and money, my fears of losing our home, and the lack of funds, led to disagreements that would never have occurred in our lives before. I had stopped caring what he thought of me. The Husband gave in to his drinking and mental depression, and I started to become the one who made some of the decisions, causing our old relationship to morph into a "woman doing more than was her right," according to church regulations. However, during this transformation, I discovered my independence, an independence I clung to. I stopped having to ask permission to go somewhere; stopped explaining my life to someone who wasn't interested.

Love requires respect, and I no longer respected the man who chose to be a drunkard. Without respect and trust, love cannot grow. Not that I could show him a lack of respect. That would be dangerous and against my religion, but there it was, blooming in my heart and mind. When I asked if he'd look for work, he turned on me, claiming I had no idea what it took to work in the world. It was true I had never been allowed to get *a real job*. He didn't consider art a job.

"Maybe you should give it a try," he sneered.

That became my ticket. I proposed a bet: whoever got a real job first would go to work.

Two days later, I was hired by a company as a housekeeper. The Husband would need to stay home with the kids.[6] Was I worried? Yes. But I felt more terrified of homelessness, so I counted on whatever love he had left for his sons to make him rise to the occasion. I had to believe he would take better responsibility and drink less when I wasn't there. My dad had been a drinker. As a child, I was accustomed to seeing him being pushed into the bedroom by my mom to get him out of sight. I used to hear my parents arguing. My father's drinking never seemed to prevent him from working. I was determined to provide for my family, and this determination gave me the strength to take this step.

It created a broader crack in our relationship, which caused us to careen wildly down the path of destruction. A new part of my life began to materialize.

Later, I learned, much to my overwhelming sadness, that I could have been charged with child neglect for leaving them with a "sick" father.[7] But, back then, there was no one to tell me. The families knew he was a drunkard, and no one said a thing. It all felt normal. His abuse had morphed into quiet neglect. Sure, he threw tantrums when things didn't go his way, but he never laid a hand on our sons. They'd learned to fend for themselves in my absence, making their own sandwiches and figuring out what to do with their day. But it weighed on me every time I went out the door.

His drinking had become such an everyday part of our lives. I had no one to question whether this had happened in other homes or just mine. Did I find out years later that I was as much a betrayer to my children as he was because I hadn't chosen better, done better, left the marriage earlier, or fixed everything somehow? Because I couldn't get him to stop drinking? Perhaps I should have poured out more wine bottles, attended even more Al-Anon meetings, and read even more self-help books than I had?

For God's sake, shouldn't I have just been fucking brave enough to rip off my superhero cape and mask, which I wore trying to save— save—*save* this marriage, and just bailed out, saving myself and my sons? Yes, my shame and sadness still follow me. Nothing I tried worked, and God did not save us. We had not saved ourselves.

So, I went to work.

Cleaning other people's dirt

I cleaned with such dedication and vigor that clients wanted me exclusively, which became a problem for the company, as there was only one of me. Things happen to you when you scrub other people's floors and toilets, when people living their privilege feel socially above their housekeepers. Some had me enter through their back doors to let me know I was "the hired help," and lower on the social scale. Some wanted me to cook a meal, or watch their children while cleaning, which was not part of my job. Sometimes I ended up cleaning the whole house on my own because the other housekeeper went behind closed doors to serve clients in a way I felt did not align with my moral standards. Later, after learning all their rules about running a housekeeping business, I built my own business, scrubbing my way to independence.

Money plays a significant role in a relationship's power dynamic. Eventually, The Husband grew tired of being at home and returned to a low-paying job repairing copy machines. He attended an IT college and had to complete some classes to get a degree. I helped him with some of those subjects and assisted with his homework, as some were too difficult or uninteresting for him. I was unwilling to give up my job, so I continued to work. My boys were getting old enough to be home alone, and were at school for most of the day.

For the first time in their lives, their mom would not be home with cookies baked. Their dad was not home either. My youngest son was the first to be home alone, for about 45 minutes. He was old enough but he admitted he was scared, which broke my heart. I found him a talking "Alf" doll at the thrift store, that still worked. He dragged it around the house with him, making it talk to him over and over until his brothers came home, and I not long after.

And Then There Were Drugs

One day, The Husband and I had a terrible altercation over the checkbook and checking account. I had opened and read the bank statement out of curiosity (something I had never done before, as it had remained in his exclusive domain) and saw that he was withdrawing a staggering amount of money each day, declaring it was for his lunch. In what world does a single lunch cost that much? That much money would buy our groceries for a week! Our argument continued, and it turned out, to my horror, that he admitted to delving drugs, as well as his drinking problem.[8]

He tossed the checkbook at me and said, "Fine, you deal with the money then."

I knew little to nothing about managing accounts or handling money. He still took whatever he wanted. At least I now understood why we were so poor and how little he cared for his family. It was right there on the bank statement in black and white.

The wife of his buddy at work called out of the blue one day, exclaiming, "You'd better keep your husband home!" They had both created a fire in her husband's garage, while concocting drugs in there at three in the morning. Her husband had been burned. My mouth folded in a hopeless frown. *As if I could ever make The Husband do anything. I was shocked to hear this new twist of trouble for our lives.* How much more of a statistic did our lives have to become?

My religion taught that we should marry in the church and not be unequally yoked with an unbeliever. The Husband had faded away from the church, which had scared and confused me. I felt more lost and less like a *"Chosen One"* than ever before. God had turned his back on my sons and me. We didn't discuss his new habits, or what they would mean for our lives. It was a new level of terror.

I had done all the things that dysfunctional wives do when their drunken husband requests them, like calling his work when he was too sick to come in and throwing blankets over him wherever he passed out in the house for the night. I walked into stores under his duress to buy bottles for him because he was too ill and drunk to walk in there and get them himself. He would cry desperately and shake from lack of alcohol. I reassured him that no spiders were crawling on the walls or snakes on the floor, as we were equally terrified of the warped reality we lived in and what was happening to us all. But I finally gathered courage and stopped all of that, telling him I would no longer participate in his personal dysfunction anymore. The crack in the teacup of our marriage opened fully, and the tea spilled.

The sadness piled up. The grief of my life became too heavy and difficult. As I put my hands in soapy water while cleaning someone else's dirt, I paused and wondered, *How this had become my life? I thought I had done everything right, as the Church had said, but look at our lives.* How were people like my sons and me supposed to survive?

During the most challenging times, the darkest thoughts crept in again, thoughts that maybe I would be better off dead than living this way. These terrible thoughts didn't just drive me out of love with The Husband. They pushed me far from God. Somewhere deep inside, I believed I had sinned by overstepping The Husband and that God had thus left me alone in the mess I had chosen.

A punishment, the ultimate punishment.

The hopeless hell of my life, the grueling labor I did outside the home, and all of the work waiting inside it, left me very little time to do anything but survive.

We eventually had to leave this house and move again to another one.

Note to reader: In today's market, if a man had to pay for every single thing a wife quietly does, cooking, cleaning, caring, managing household life, he'd be writing checks rivaling a professional's salary. Contracting full-time homemaker services in the U.S. can cost close to **$70,000 a year**, and globally, the unpaid care and domestic work done largely by women is valued at nearly **$11 trillion annually.**[8] *The irony, of course, is that homemakers are never paid that rate themselves; it's simply what it would cost to replace their labor on the open market.*

"Freeing yourself was one thing, claiming ownership of that freed self was another."

~Toni Morrison

Chapter Eleven

House of Changing Wind

That Morning

Every year, all it takes is for the air to crisp, and the September ground to shiver with the beginning of fall, to make me remember the dying.

I carefully placed my bare feet among the forest floor debris, but even so, my steps rustled loudly, and a cold sweat trickled down my back. The noise could wake the sleeping Husband.

I would be discovered in my sneaking. There was no time to change clothes or be extra careful. I closed my eyes for a moment, licking my dry lips. My cautious walking brought me to just beneath our bedroom window, one story up. I heard panting and was shocked to realize it came from me. Hunched over, I felt the terror rippling through my body, every nerve on fire, with one thought spinning in my mind: *What if he feels my terror in his sleep?*

He knew.

I knew he had felt the changing wind just as I had. Last evening, he had been like a standing grizzly bear, squinting and sniffing about, unsure of where the danger lay, as we talked.

The Critic, that loud voice in my mind, hissed at me about how silly I would look if he caught me doing this. *What possible explanation will you give? Will you lie again? Go on and add that sin too.*

Yes, I had lied. Not outright, but with omission and deflection. *Don't admit you left the property with the boys to walk the bike trail. If he asks for your opinion during intimacy, only say positive things.* It was what I had to do to be safe. Disagreement had never been allowed; it stood as one of the greatest rules. The Critic pressed harder: *You're going to mess this up, too.*

Why had I come up on this side of the house? Where had my common sense gone? My mind flicked like a frantic TV remote, flashing jagged snapshots of our life. I was about to end that life *because the boys had asked for this.* The Husband had seemed content with how things were, so I had to become the changing wind.

My throat went dry. My hands shook. Terror threatened to freeze me in place. Yesterday I had stashed some belongings in the basement storage. I had already put my four sons' getaway bags into the car. There hadn't been time for my own. I grabbed my bag now, stuffed in what I held, and wondered whether I could make it to the car without being caught. Tears gathered, and I pressed them back with my fingers.

He had NEVER liked crying. If he saw my tears, I'd have to explain them, and the time for talking was long over.

My Confession

My confession is that for so long, so very long, I had been "sleeping" through our life. He had been "sleeping" too. It became easier to pretend all was fine in our minds, to cushion from the pain, than to stay awake to the truth.

Days bled into each other until years piled up, buried under thick layers of marital dust. I simply rose each morning and performed my role. I moved through duties like a ghost haunting my own home. Somewhere deep inside, I knew the truth was festering, waiting, knowing it registered as the biggest lie ever:

I didn't want this life.

Not the overflowing loneliness, not the labor, not the emptiness that greeted me every dawn and tucked me in every night.

I hated it every day, all day.

I tried to convince myself that I found meaning in both my duty and my role, that they could make up for the misery.

The chafing thing about being a Christian woman is having to be better than everyone else, even though you're not. It becomes an Achilles heel. I couldn't drink myself numb or turn to drugs. I was supposed to be a "*Chosen One.*"

I couldn't run away. Just leave my family and disappear.

I couldn't stray far from the role God supposedly required.

There were no shopping trips.

No coffee shop dates.

No girlfriends at all.

My only escape became sinking "asleep" in my own mind.

But suddenly—I had been slapped violently awake.

Our sons had ripped open the curtains of our life. They held the mirror; they forced light into the room we had kept dark, and light hurts. Who would have thought it could be so painful?

Thoughts came in jagged pieces. Our lives felt like they were being poured into a blender, and none of it made much sense anymore. We were trapped in the same small circle of repeated emotions and behaviors: fear, pain, remorse, and the empty promises of "Sorry, sorry, I'll never do that again!" until the next time.

I had learned this was called the "Cycle of Violence."[1]

There wasn't a god interested in saving us, nor had we seemed able to save ourselves. We had tried counseling once or twice, but he hated the marriage counselor *he* had picked, who had seen through him. No knight in shining armor existed to ride up and save either of us.

Now, I had to be the wind that brought the change.

The checklist becomes long when you have a lifetime to end. Stepping gingerly again around twigs and leaves, I moved up toward the car, the trunk lid already cracked open the way I had left it.

"*Sneak,*" my Critic hissed. "*You haven't even told the kids. They don't even know yet, do they?*"

They had been waiting patiently for me to do something.

My sons had asked for this, to leave, to live somewhere else, even when we had nowhere to go.

That became the slap I needed to fix this mess. They said they would rather live in a field than at home with us, their parents. That was the slap.

Still, I just hadn't told them today had to be the day.

This is what it had all come to.

Already feeling ill from my efforts, I went back inside. How easy it would be to crawl back into our bed. I could still end this idea. Nobody would have to know. Ah, but that wasn't true. I had told his family, and once you say something out loud or in a letter, you must do it.

I had been afraid that I would back out.

If you stay, you will end up dying one day, never having truly lived a good life. What will become of your mind and spirit? And what will become of your sons? What are they learning from this crazy life?

Our life ignited, turning to ash as I walked through the side door.

Needing to breathe, I steadied myself, trying to calm the trembling and frantic thoughts that were vibrating with fear. I started mentally counting off things left to do, the Critic nipping at my heels. Everything felt so wrong. And why not? *I never did anything right. Wasn't that what I had been reminded of endlessly?*

I went to the kitchen first.

On the center counter sat a small gift. It was such an oddity that I just stared at it. My whole body felt a blow, as if an actual fist had landed in my center.

Why now?

Of all times, in all the years, why had he done this?

So many emotions whirled like a kaleidoscope. Their sheer rawness and heaviness made me feel as if my life could end right then, in our own kitchen. That day, our anniversary, was supposed to be my gift to myself: a day I leapt from the train wreck of our lives and tried to save my sons and me.

That's how I would celebrate it.

I could count the gifts he had given the children or me on one hand.

Why *this* day?

What I planned to do would make me so undeserving in his eyes.

I would be taking on a new role. The "quitter" and, more descriptively, the "Bitch."

"You know why he got the gift." My Critic whispered. "He feels it. He knows somehow, and he is scared."

He must have felt my resolve.

The gift was store-wrapped, which undoubtedly cost extra. Surprise fluttered in my chest. He never spent money on such things, not for me, not for the boys.

For a moment, I forgot my purpose in the kitchen. I forgot what I needed to do, just stood there blinking at the oddity on the counter as the sun began coming awake outside.

All the pain and grief in my life teetered there with me.

My crippling weakness was the teetering. *It was so easy to close my eyes and not see, to just sleep.* I have done it many times before.

But then a hot anger rose within me. It possessed my body, surged up from someplace unknown to me. This white-hot rage pushed me over the edge. I burned with it.

How dare he?

How dare he think *this* could even begin to fix this war of our lives! The wreckage we had built, piece by piece over the years, surrounded us now, evidence of the harm we'd learned to live with, holding us in a stalemate neither of us could break.

I had already become the living dead. I was sure he must have felt that way himself. He stood as the practicing alcoholic (with some drugs and smoking on the side, just to be sure he didn't have to be present). I had become the perpetual "doer"—doing, doing, doing whatever needed to be done, while keeping my head down to survive.

A recent clandestine visit to a crisis counselor, paid for with my housekeeping money, enlightened me about the dangers in my life. Just 15 minutes into my hesitant, quiet story as I fumbled through describing it with my eyes fixed on the floor, she abruptly interrupted me. *"Did you know that you could go to jail for leaving your children at home with him? If something happens, if one gets hurt, the law will see you as the responsible adult."*

I hadn't even mentioned the bad things, the shameful stuff, yet. My confusion and horror at her words left me mortified. I had lived a life dedicated to being a good Christian. Of course, I was far from perfect, but I had a goal. I tried hard to be the woman described in Proverbs 31, the one any man would be grateful to have, *except for mine.*

She recommended that I call the Domestic Violence Coalition for advice. She warned me to get a police escort because *"his type could get dangerous."*

I thought about how I had been taught that a woman is to run her house so efficiently and cleanly and that if Christ were to appear for a visit, he would be duly impressed with her efforts.

I even had a plastic recipe-card box, which we all received for free at that special church meeting for wives. A green one with cleaning tasks cards for every single day of the month to organize our household duties. I had *actually* used mine, even proudly adding the yearly things to do.

I would have been prepared for a Christ-like visitation.

But nothing had prepared me for **real life**.

Not *this* life.

Even though our religion subjugated women, they reminded us at weekly services of the importance of our role. The husband must lead in all things, and wives, of course, are to submit *in all things*. We were the chosen people. God had a plan for us. Did this plan include me going to jail?

How would any of these teachings help me now?

For years, I had believed most of the things the church taught. And if the small voice of questioning spoke in my mind, I silenced it quickly so I would not become a heretic. These were the people I had grown up with, and I had a place and community here. Although I did not share my life story with them, I could sit among them every Saturday and feel a sense of belonging.

As I sat in the counselor's office, all the sacrifice and suffering pressed against my throat, choking out my words. I was brimming over with fear and anger.

"He," the counselor said, "is considered sick, as alcoholism is an illness." And I stood as the supposed sane, functional adult who *had* (presumably) left the children with a drunk.

So, the law would support *him*, not me.

My whole life felt shattered in that moment.

I hadn't come this far to end up in jail for a man I no longer respected, a man for whom any remaining feelings had long since unraveled. Our life together was like a tapestry whose threads had been pulled out one by one until nothing recognizable remained. The old threads looped through every part of our lives, our homes, our children, our memories, until the knot of it was too tangled to undo.

One stubborn thread still clung to my heart, making that day ache in ways I could barely endure.

I left her office in a daze.

The counselor had helped me make an exit plan, one that I had barely enough courage for. With no family to take me in and no friends to fall back on, I appeared to be walking off the edge of the plank into nowhere.

Ah! But Back to the Kitchen

I was shocked at how much anger a dead person could feel. I had been simmering with anger for some time, unaware of the havoc it had caused. I did not even understand the reasons behind my anger. I knew I couldn't show Him my rage, not ever. It wasn't worth the price. But I could show the kids, which I had unwittingly done.

Of course, I didn't mean to. I wasn't angry with them. I was only angry with myself, The Husband, and life in general. I was appalled at the *fine mess* we were living in, a home so full of unhappiness that my sons became conspirators, planning their escape. They were leaving us. Worse, in my mind, they were leaving *me*. I had been clueless about their pain.

Back in the kitchen, I stared at the gift sitting there, closed my eyes, and held onto the counter to keep from swaying.

Just a Few Months Back

Our life hadn't really been that bad, had it? This thought wove through my mind as I looked at all my sons' sober little faces. Had it been so awful for them? They had never complained to me. I thought we had been good at keeping the dirty laundry in the hamper and shielding them from the worst. But then, hadn't we all watched the same drunk, his rampages and blackouts?

Wasn't it the boys who wanted me to go out at 3 a.m. to look for him while he drank away from home, frantic with childhood fear and indignant with me?

When he had passed out in the front yard, and we couldn't even move him, I covered him with a blanket. We all went back inside, looking at each other with worry and fear of what he would do the next morning.

They didn't even want to stay home with him during the day, but I had to go to work and clean houses. I wasn't working for fun. There was never enough money, even for basics. They tiptoed around their dad, their eyes filled with lost childhood dreams, doing for themselves whenever possible.

Now older, they told me they were leaving, going, running away without me. They had watched my face like little hawks as I crumpled into tears, as the full weight of what they were saying crushed me.

I thought I had kept them safe from it all, tucked them into routines and some fun moments, and shielded them by trying to do more. But children know the sound of a sinking ship, even when you play music over the creaking.

My confusion puzzled them, maybe because they expected resistance or anger. My oldest son, serious and soft-spoken, who now a teen, said clearly and determinedly, *"We are ready to live in a field rather than live here with our dad."*

(And *you* ... by association—became the unspoken truth.)

He added sternly, *"We are leaving."*

I was speechless as I looked over the four of them and saw the truth in their faces. Feeling sorry for me, one of the younger boys asked his brothers if I could come too.

If I hadn't been broken before by their words, this silent debate they had between themselves, with their eyes, shattered me, making me fully awake to the fallout we had made of our lives.

They didn't even want me!

This knowledge brought me to my knees.

My own sons didn't want me!

I knew my boys well enough to know that one day I would come home, and they would all be gone, even though they had never camped out for a day in their lives and had no money, or place to go.

All this time, I had wrapped myself in the belief that I was doing the right thing by staying and holding together a marriage I thought God expected me to keep. I had worked hard, sacrificed much, and convinced myself I was building something noble out of the wreckage.

But at that moment, I saw the truth: I had not created a good life for them; I had only contributed to it as a prisoner of my own making.

Their words cut through my slumber. While grief and shame wrapped around my heart like a noose, something else rose stronger— **love.**

I loved my sons more than my marriage, more than a need to be *"right"* or *"chosen,"* more than the rules that had kept me shackled.

That was the moment I chose them.

That was the moment I chose to change everything.

Anger, fear, and sadness filled every nook and cranny of my being. No amount of faith, hope, or prayer could save us now. Since the beginning, He had chosen to drown in the lake of his desire for alcohol and drugs. So many times, I had put on the cape and superhero mask, trying to save him and prevent him from dragging us down as well.

Each time I pulled us from a disaster once more, we lay back on the shore of life, wet with tears, exhausted, and confused.

We would get through all the drama, the flailing, the crying, the silence, the resentment, the pain, the anger, and the forgiveness, and then, it would start all over again.

I had drowned in all of that for years. My knees were sore from kneeling to pray for salvation for us all. My body had folded and refolded so many times, trying to pretzel into being what he wanted. I no longer knew who I had become.

Perhaps if I had prayed from my true voice, not the one trained to please the church, not the one bound by spiritual expectations, I would have whispered:

Please help me find the door.

Help me save my children.

Help me save myself.

Not the marriage, not the role, not to keep up appearances, but to save *us*.

We were drowning in something that could never be healed by pretending it was holy. I'd been praying from the wrong mouth all along, the mouth trained to recite what sounded righteous. But what if I had spoken from the mouth of my aching heart, the one that said:

I want out.

I want peace.

I want my children to have a better life.

Would God have answered me differently if I had finally spoken the truth aloud?

No Awards for Last Place

I would never win the "Awesome Mother of the Year Award," even though I thought I had been trying so, so very hard. Everything I did and suffered was to be that good mom and wife. In my mind, my sons needed at least one parent to try, yet I still had failed. A wasted, ridiculous life was what I saw behind me.

As if that wasn't enough, a teacher, concerned about my youngest son, phoned me. Her conversation left me dazed and disheartened.

My youngest son wanted to die. He sat at his desk all day, staring into space or sleeping, and participated little in class. He drew pictures of skeletons and depictions of death and dying. There were so many "red flags" here that she had referred him to a school counselor.

"Your son is talking about suicide, *Mrs. Supermom*, but I wouldn't worry too much at this point; the counselor had said that at his young age, he doesn't even know how to accomplish the feat. When he is a teen, though, you will have a problem. Is there anything going on at home, *Mrs. Supermom*?" You could hear the proverbial pin drop.

Yes.

I had built a house on the sand, and now the high tide had come.

The crumbling became steady after that. I saw it daily, painfully aware of our life blinking in my eyes.

It amazed me that the Alcoholic listened to the same warning I brought home from the school meeting, then just bought another bottle, rolled over to "sleep," and carried on as if nothing needed to change.

He lived as if he existed in a motel, where everything miraculously happened for him, clothes and meals delivered as requested. He had little to give back, not sharing his obvious pain or struggles with us. His lifestyle consumed him. If a problem arose, it fell to me to resolve it.

There were mental-health appointments, questions, sessions, turmoil, and more fear. Back then, I had no close friends, who could have been friends with me in the life we had? Years later, I found a couple of neighbors I started to confide in. I had actually asked them if leaving my marriage could be morally wrong, if divorce was that evil. It showed how unsure I had become of my own "true north."

So many times, I had tried to believe in myself, but I had been talked out of it by The Husband's authoritative knowledge, his parents, or the church. There was no talking to my parents.

I needed someone to listen to me!

The crux of the matter was this: leaving The Husband wasn't done in the religion that ruled my life. The church excommunicated people right and left for infractions of the laws, and it had been all I knew in those days, the one place I was allowed to go besides grocery stores and, later, my work.

My mom had set a fine example of weathering abuse and honoring her commitments, eventually outliving her abuser. Neither of our families knew many details of our lives for various reasons, but they were indeed aware of our problems. They knew He drank nearly all the time. The message I heard was that it's socially improper to interfere in other people's adult lives; they (we) needed to fix it ourselves.

The boys were still waiting for me, watching with expectant eyes. I had asked them to give me time to "make a plan" and to talk to the experts who helped people escape, but everything started crumbling so fast that the ground became slippery.

At that moment, there I stood in our kitchen, teetering over this decision, my toes poised on a cliff's edge.

That Morning, Still in the Kitchen

The sun streamed into the kitchen, cutting shapes of light through the window slats and patterning across the room, where I still stood, frozen. The time, oh my god! The time! It became almost too late to stop all of this if I had even wanted to.

I jolted into motion, waking the boys, frantic to follow the plan. We would make it look like we were going to church as usual. On some Saturdays, when we could, we would go just to get away. If the Alcoholic tried to stop us, I would have a righteous reason to leave him, as in our faith, the right to attend church was God given.

If The Husband blocked it, I would have the right to leave him, but I could never marry again. Marriage could be a cage you entered only once, and death released you. And our marriage had become slavery. The other way to be totally free of this whole mess is if he no longer wanted me. He had told me clearly that if I ever left, he would hurt me and/or see to it that I'd never get the boys.

Leaving had become a very frightening thing to do.

The DVC (Domestic Violence Coalition) counselor I had called suggested I get a police escort for safety. "His type," they warned me again, "could be violent." I thought, *What do they know of my husband?* So, I chose to ask his brother or his mother to come instead, considering it a small kindness, something I could offer him. Maybe it would soften him, even after everything was said and done.

The boys needed showering, dressing, and breakfast.

How had the time slipped away?

I rushed to get ready, my heart pounding. Then one of the boys shouted: ***"Grandma is outside!"***

No! NO!

They were too early, and The Husband had woken up, coming down the hall, his eyes pinned to mine, sharp, alert.

He felt the wind then, as it rushed through the house.

They had arrived earlier than I had requested. I had planned to be gone before they arrived, leaving only a letter behind. Talking to him never worked, when his answering anger came in the form of flying objects or smashed walls.

There was never emotional maturity between us.

There were no late-night talks.

There was no safety in honesty.

There was no warm-hearted laughter or joking moments.

Tearing out my pink sponge curlers, I ran my fingers through my hair, my mind screaming, ***"What do I do now?"***

He walked toward me. I never wanted to see the look on his face, which was equal parts confusion, betrayal, and rage.

"You're leaving me, aren't you?"

My mouth wouldn't form words, but my face betrayed me.

I did not have a plan B.

Like a crazy movie, I found myself participating in scenes as if I were in an actual stop-action movie directed by someone else. Moments unfolded in slow motion, and a haze of fear and numbing emotions enveloped me.

His brother, meaning well, thought it best that we "talk out" our problems. I barely remember walking, but he herded my enraged husband and me into the bedroom, shutting the door on us. Someone shouted that they were taking the boys out of the house, *as the prophecy had foretold*. All my mind could process were the words:

Taking the boys!

Taking the boys!

Just as The Husband had constantly threatened.

A live wire of self-preservation snapped awake inside me. Talk? There could be no more talking, for God's sake. Talk about what? There were no more words that hadn't been said in some way or another during those drowning years. No more actions that hadn't been tried.

I can't explain how much his family's act of interference hurt me so deeply and profoundly at that moment. Their well-intentioned actions put me in harm's way. And according to the DVC experts, we were all in harm's way.

The Husband had become *Anger,* distilled and pure. He frightened and sobered me into stillness, even though my mind screamed *get away, get away!* I had previously thought he was capable of killing me, but right then and there, I thought he might actually do it!

He radiated thoughts into the air: anger, hate, pain. His hard eyes stared at me, his face flushed, livid in purple and red. He was in his full grizzly form.

Hate and pain flashed out of his eyes and into his bellowing words, thrown at me from where he stood. I stood buffeted by the storm of his disbelief and anger.

He stood glaring, holding onto the gift he had earlier snatched off the counter, suddenly shoved it into my face, and barked:

"I bought it for you!" (*Ungrateful woman implied.*)

He said it with disgust and demanded I open it. So, with shaking fingers, I did.

He demanded I read the card aloud to him, and I did.

My terrorized self did anything he asked.

It sat in my palm, torn from its beautiful paper, an oversized coffee cup with a terrible, grimacing cartoon face on it that said, "Stressed Out?"

I stood there frozen. Did he really think all of the pain of our lives would go away with a gift? With a coffee cup? There were no words for the absurdity, the ridiculousness of it, the desperation of the moment. I could not move. I just stared at my first real anniversary present.

The mug, balanced in the palm of my hand, wavered out in front of me like an offering left at an altar. It was hideous, loud, and clumsy. I didn't want it. It wasn't a gift, not really, but a placeholder for all the years of silence, a last-ditch bribe disguised as effort.

It felt like the kind of thing someone gives when they feel the ground shifting beneath them, hoping a trinket might keep the walls from crumbling. But I had already crumbled. No gift could rebuild what we had allowed to decay. *I did not take the bait this time.*

I set it on the bed, and I turned toward my sons, my truth, my choice.

He saw it in my face as I turned to leave.

Suddenly, he dropped to the floor in his grief and grabbed my ankles, holding tight and crying out for me not to leave him, to give him (yet another) chance.

Babbling spilled from his mouth about buying me a red sports car, about more things I had never cared about or wanted. I felt stuck in a terrible movie. This could not be happening.

There I stood, shocked, surprised, and uncomfortable at his display of emotion. That he would be down on his knees in such a debased position, gripping me, someone whom he had reminded often wasn't good enough and never did anything right.

Why did he even want me when I no longer wanted him? *We no longer wanted him.*

The "movie of our life" paused then, showing me wracked with guilt for being the cause of all this, him crying at my feet, holding my ankles.

I heard a Bible scripture, in my mind: "They shall reap what they sow," and so we were.

I declared this the most terrible moment of my life so far, and there had been many contenders. I thought I heard the actual tearing of fabric. The "quilt" that had been our lives, woven with all the moments, the years, and snapshots of our days, had its threads torn with a rending so loud that the neighbors must have heard it, too.

I just needed to be out of there. I had to get away, be anywhere but here. The very air smelled of scorched words, broken hearts, and dreams. Instinctively, I knew he would hate me even more for having debased himself at my feet. I had to flee, so I did. It appeared to be the only skill I had at that moment.

In my sleepwear, I drove to a park bathroom and changed into clothes that I had stashed in the trunk. They had my children! All my thoughts in my frightened mind funneled into:

They had taken my children!
Just like he always said they would!

If he stayed in the home and kept the boys, what would become of me? All of this had been for them. They had wanted this the most from the start, and I was along for the ride, catching the momentum. Somewhere in my head, I had known his family had removed the kids from the battlefield, but I was beyond the ability to think and reason, crazed with fear and indecision. So even though I stood as a grown woman, I did what any girl does when she becomes a brokenhearted lost woman: I called my dad from a pay phone.

In my frantic tears and sobs, I told him what had happened. I asked my dad what I should do. In absolute anger, my father said I should talk it out, settle things, and start over, but I knew he didn't understand. He didn't know. He had never known.

I would rather have died than go back to that life. I had never spoken of the choking, the raping, the punched holes in the walls, of being locked up, of having no food. How can you tell a parent such things? How could I have told anyone? Even the counselor didn't know all of this.

Then, I called our minister, the leader of all our lives, the voice of God. I thought I would ask him not to let my husband's family take my children, as I genuinely believed they would.

Hadn't it been predicted?

Finally, the minister picked up the call. Ah! In hysterics by then (a curious place to be if you have never been), I had shouted into the phone, *"They took my boys and made me go into the bedroom with HIM."*

I tried to explain (where had they taken the boys?) I didn't know; I had been too frightened to hear that. To my disappointment, the pastor also suggested I return, but I could not go back to that house or that family. I could not suffer them trying to convince me to stay again.

I don't even remember everything I did, where I went, or how I knew when it became safe for me to return. All the memories are lost in the spin of time and fear.

In that moment, I realized something massive: My father and the minister, the two greatest authorities beyond The Husband, could only offer the rules they themselves had been handed. They saw the role, not the woman standing before them unraveling.

I was reaching for help and seeking answers as my plan (which, granted, hadn't been a good one) fell apart. I felt lost and scared, unsure of what to do next. All I found were voices shaped by patriarchy, voices that had never really seen me. They only saw who they thought I should be, not the full humanity of me, a person wanting a safer, kinder life.

Someone who was now breaking apart under the weight and silence of her marriage. But none of their words had helped.

I would have to find my own words, my own voice, and my own way out.

The Night Before all of this

We never talked in the way I supposed other people might. He wasn't interested in what I thought, wanted, or needed. Our conversations consisted of me being told what to do, receiving criticism, or attempting to say something non-threatening to solve a problem. I could never be sure what, if anything, I said would set him off. There were so many unspoken rules.

Of course, the church had a monopoly on rules, but our relationship also had its own set too. The boys and I had carefully learned them, to get through each day as safely as possible. Sometimes, the rules did change, making life even more complicated, and I had broken a rule tonight.

I had gone off to sit alone.

He always wanted to know where I was.

The Husband came to find me on the back porch. The hair on my neck prickled. He didn't usually look for me at this time of day. His drinking often had him close to passing out by now, but tonight, he seemed sober, which felt so much worse.

I could feel finality in the air.

I had been thinking about our "ending" and my plan of action for the next day, while perched on the porch steps, terrified he could catch the scent of it on me. We sat awkwardly together but far apart on our back deck. Togetherness had always been stressful for us.

How can my truth ever be spoken in this world?

We both stared out into the landscape.

The country club golf course stretched before us. We couldn't use it; we were renters and considered second-class annoyances with children. I had become a house cleaner for many of the members in this gated community, working eight hours a day.

Still, we were fortunate to have a beautiful view. Sometimes, wild turkeys and deer would wander onto the greens as the golfers left. Beyond it, mountains speckled with pines and oaks were painted in a sunset of golden orange and pink.

My eyes took in the sight as if I would never see such beauty again, because I didn't know where I would be at the next sunset.

Letters had been written and sent to his folks and mine. I had done this, so I could not back out without more shame. I mentally ticked off parts of my idea of how we would leave.

He sat still and silent, busy with his smoking. He never knew how much his silence hurt, almost as much as his criticism. What did he feel about us? What did he want? Our silences were not a gentle hum between two people who could quietly listen; they were like the stillness before the storm.

"What are we going to do?" He asked into the quiet, not looking my way ("about us" hung in the air, unspoken.) The emotional teeter-totter

always started when he talked, lifting my hope one moment, dropping it the next. He spoke of things that made it sound like we might make it. But I could not, would not, hear it tonight.

I remember saying I didn't know and feeling the sour taste of the lie. I wanted to scream, *"There is no us!"* But my thoughts were like stones. If I opened my mouth to finally speak my truths, they would all fall out in a landslide that would bury us both.

There I sat, planning to quit the next day, on our anniversary.

Nausea and despair filled me.

I couldn't bear the thought of living through another year of this, and my sons, in their quiet bravery, had made it clear they couldn't either.

In the beginning, he had offered just enough scraps to make me believe it was love. But that hope no longer found purchase in my heart.

The trees were now black silhouette shapes against the sky, and I sat still, perched on the wooden steps where the chill of the night crept under my clothes. We never touched, moving past each other like repelling ends of magnets. If he had just opened up, been real for once, maybe he could have sat beside me and held me. Perhaps if he looked into my face and spoke from his heart, I could have begun to believe and fanned the flames of love I had once felt for him.

But as always, we were like warriors glancing at one another from across the battlefield, his sword and my shield at the ready.

He started to talk, saying that neither he nor I could or should just quit. (Did he know of my plans?) I began to suspect his family had said something to him.

My mind wanted to tumble out years of pent-up words piled up behind my lips. Words about the pain and suffering, loneliness, and the god-awful disaster we had come to, but here he sat, speaking softly as if we were okay and somehow, we would make it.

He didn't see the same picture of our lives as I did.

I realized he never would, not as long as the bottle still sat in his hand.

I remembered how much I had loved him at the beginning, how much I had tried to hold on to that feeling. I wasn't sure when it disappeared, buried under layers of our strange and awful life.

Afterward, In the Wreckage

When the dust settled from our breakup, it covered everything inches thick. My biggest fear of hurting people and doing wrong came true.

In the train wreck we had created, I may not have said everything right, done everything in the best way, or even remembered it precisely as it happened that terrible day. I remember the terror and the trembling in me as I let go of everything I had ever known.

One of us had to try to save what remained of us, and that's what I did. I took off the cape and mask of my "super-heroism," left them on the shore, and walked away, with my sons, and at last, with myself.

I never looked back.

My mother-in-law, who in the beginning had been my only allowed "friend" for most of my married days, phoned me chidingly as if I were a misbehaving child. Her voice crackled with anger. She was livid that I had accused them of taking my children away from me (had I said that? I must have, my panic was so loud I barely remembered the words) and furious that I had "run off like that." (That part, I did). But worst of all, I had spoken to someone outside the FAMILY.

How could I? How *dare* I?

I could tell she felt extremely distraught, and I had been well-trained. I knew the crime of arguing with an angry person, especially someone who held power. So, I pushed the phone tighter to my ear, closed my eyes, and listened. I deserved this, didn't I?

Her voice tugged up old memories of my father from years ago, when he had told me never to discuss our family business with anyone but him. A difficult task, considering he had been the primary source of my problems.

But something shifted that day. My mother-in-law's words raised the hair on the back of my neck.

How dare she.

She had turned her eyes from the truth of my life. She had thanked me for "taking care" of her son many times, but never once validated the damage it had caused to me, or her grandchildren. I remember thinking: **Someday I will speak my truth, the one none of you has ever wanted to hear.**

She went on to say I had gotten upset that day merely because I "didn't get things my way." Such a familiar accusation. She said she was disappointed in me and that she had tried to help us save our marriage by stopping my departure.

I felt a snap in my body. Our so-called friendship was severed forever in that instant.

For years, his parents had told me that if I left him, *he would quit drinking*. They said it as if it were a promising outcome. But now that I had done exactly that, I was the villain, the pariah. That he was not drinking *that minute* meant nothing. Once an alcoholic, always an alcoholic, The Husband had confessed to me.

I had lost so much, it seemed, for the price of freedom.

The boys were eventually brought home. They'd been taken to a deli or a coffee shop, but I didn't know that at the time. The Alcoholic had gathered a few belongings and left to stay with his parents. Later, I always suspected the deeper part of their anger towards me came from this: I had stopped caretaking him, and now he had come back to *them:* bottle, drugs, and all. I rather doubt he told them the truth of our lives, or what kind of man he had become.

They were in for a surprise.

I was allowed to stay in the home, but only for the boys. They made that very clear. They didn't want to disrupt the children's lives, pull them from school, or make them move, and for that, I felt a strange and complicated gratitude. But their kindness had conditions. They told me plainly that I did *not* deserve it. This wasn't "for me."

I knew how their family worked. You were either *In* or *Out*, and once you were Out, you became the subject of snide comments, cheap jokes, and whispered scorn.

I was "Out" now.

There is no greater hate than Christian love, after all.

She called me one more time, after that, out of the blue. Her voice had softened but not warmed. She told me she was "now doing her son's laundry and packing his lunch" as if these were some great acts of sacrifice. As if I hadn't done that every single day of my marriage when he needed it, when we had food.

What a strange thing to confess to me.

What stories had he been telling?

Who did they think held our life together with both hands for so long?

The Gambit

I had taken a risk with this idea of leaving. The gamble? I had no place to go and no real plan, hoping for a *possible* outcome.

I had lived with The Husband long enough to know he would never leave if I had told him to. If I had asked him to, more horrible memories would have piled up.

In the letter I left for him, I wrote that *I* had decided to leave. That he could keep all our thrift store belongings, everything except for my personal items and the boys' things. I knew he did not want me out there in the *world*. Wasn't that why he had locked us in at the last property, chained the gate shut? It was something I hadn't even understood at the time—that such a thing was a crime.[2]

And the kids?

Oh, he didn't want to take care of them. That would have cut into his drinking time and required effort. He would have passed the work on to his mother and family.

But it was such a fine-edged risk. He *might* have decided to keep the boys anyway. Or what if they did run away, not even wanting to be with me? I could not envision a life without them. They were all I had left, and we had become a team inside our dysfunction.

What happened was exactly what we needed:

He left us in peace and gave himself the time to try to be sober.

That evening, I sat in the "dust" with the kids, tears in their eyes. They had seen things I had never wanted them ever to see: their dad crying and packing his things. They had watched the reaper reap.

When his family intervened, something in me broke. They had never asked what was happening inside our marriage, never wondered what we were going through behind closed doors. If they had known the truth... *how could they have pushed me into a room with him and taken my children away?* When I tried to talk about our problems, it was always something I wasn't doing right or doing enough of. I felt that what they did to change my plan wasn't just misguided, it was dangerous. And the worst part? The boys weren't supposed to witness any of it.

I think now about the anger I carried in our life before, like a slow leak inside me: quiet, corrosive and unnoticed until it had seeped into the cracks of everything I loved. I didn't scream or throw things as The Husband did, but my silence hardened. Exhaustion and bitterness twisted my voice. There were times I snapped at my sons, not because of what they did but because I was drowning and didn't know how to say it out loud.

I didn't understand that pain withheld becomes pain passed on.

While I didn't mean to aim at them, I see now that my reactions taught them to brace or silence themselves. The tension in our home never truly left, even when it *seemed* calm.

That's what I own.

I didn't cause *all* the damage of that train wreck life, but I added to it. And that truth is mine to face. It is a sorrowful kind of love I hold now, hoping one day my sons will understand that we were all doing the best we could with what we had been taught. Each of us, in our own broken way, was trying to survive and trying to love.

That evening we wandered around the house, now emptied of the man we had feared but loved in our own complicated ways. I don't recall us discussing the day at all. We were like ghosts. I wished we could have checked in with each other and spoken aloud about what we had seen and felt. But I think we were afraid and stunned. Even if this was what we wanted, it was still overwhelming.

That night, we felt grateful for our beds. Things could have been so much worse.

And together, we listened to the silence of our new life.

Chapter Twelve

Freedom

We spent the night alone for the first time, without The Husband, and my sons and I slept in exhaustion and peace. I woke up to find my bed full of boys; they had wandered in during the night, their hearts full of worry, fear, and doubt.

We had never felt free to laugh, scream, and play when The Husband was home. We had to be quiet constantly, but at this moment, with all of us in the big bed together, our hair in various states of "bed head," and our hearts needing release, *we laughed.*

We laughed at everything and nothing at all. Laughter erupted from us, louder and louder, and even the dog joined in barking and romping on the bed.

Then, the last missing boy ran into the room, his eyes wide with panic. "Shut up!" he hissed, looking frantically around, his spiky hair flopping side to side with worry carved across his face. "You have to be quiet! Dad will have a fit with this noise!"

We all instantly froze, seeing and hearing his fear, a fear still inside all of us. But somehow, for some inexplicable reason, that made it even funnier! We burst into even more peals of laughter, louder than before.

"Dad's gone; don't you remember?" one of the boys shouted.

A moment of embarrassing silence gripped us, a moment when everything paused.

Then we all laughed harder again, seeing the truth dawn on the scolding boy's face.

How could any of us have forgotten *yesterday?*

This boy, too, joined the ruckus.

We had the best morning in years.

We all ran through the house in our freedom, laughing, shouting, and making as much noise as we wanted, releasing the tension and sadness that had lived in us for so long.

I kissed the walls in my joy, declaring I would do better with my life, with our lives.

Part of me wanted to retreat to my old pattern, still shadowed by fear of the unknown and the magnitude of what I had done. But when I carefully searched inside for regret… I found none.

This felt so right. For me, for us.

All our memories were of disappointment, his drinking, his rages, and our nothingness. So little good ever had space in our minds.

Price of Freedom

Freedom comes with a price. Everything fell on me then, except the rent, which The Husband or his family still paid. I worked even harder cleaning homes to pay for everything else we needed. I never phoned him or his family. Why would I? What would I say? I never knew if the boys talked to him. I never asked.

My family knew that The Husband and I were separated because of the letter I sent, but they never got too involved and did not visit. Part of me wondered if they were gloating. They had predicted this from the very beginning, with the cruelest words, having never liked him. That silence was another kind of ache.

In our church, divorce was not acceptable. I did not attend church much afterward, walking the aisles as a pariah felt difficult. It might have split the church down the middle, those for my family and those for his family, and I could not bear to see any of them. I couldn't stand to see their faces, hopeful for fresh gossip, and have my life tossed into the chicken yard again to be pecked over.

The first time the Alcoholic phoned me, I already knew he would. The DVC organization had carefully advised me that he would call, and he would threaten to kill himself *if I didn't take him back.* They stated this with solid assurance.

I wasn't sure. I couldn't imagine him saying such a thing.

But they were right.

I had carefully listened to precisely what they said to do.

I was terrified. I feared he would talk his way back into our lives, that I'd wobble and give in. I dreaded the thought of him showing up at the door, forcing me to see the face I had once loved. More than anything, I feared he'd wedge himself back into the life I was trying so hard to reclaim.

When he finally called, he sounded like a small boy, frightened and crying. He felt afraid and said so. The silence stretched between us.

Steeling myself against his pain and his needs became the second hardest thing I had to do. My boys and I had to come first, or all of this had been for nothing. I felt wicked and cruel, straining to keep my tone plain and emotionless. He never really understood how far removed I had grown from him. Each day, I got up without a thought of him, having done what I had done to be away from him.

Reforming him wasn't part of the plan anymore. Those days were long past.

He could live his life any way he liked, as long as he stayed away from me. If the boys wanted to see him, of course, they could. They never asked me to take them to visit him. Not once.

On that phone call, he said the exact words, *the exact words* that DVC had said he would: "If you don't take me back, I'll kill myself!"

My stomach twisted, but I repeated the words they had taught me to say, reciting them like a script written to save my life.

"I'm so sorry if that's what you choose to do, but it's your choice."

A harsh yet effective thing to say to someone.

He responded in his old way of cruel, spiteful name-calling, His tears drying up quickly. He never understood the loss of my feelings for him, nor could He accept it in the moment. He thought there had to be another man.

He didn't know how hard it felt for me to say all of that. How hard it was not to be swept back by the same familiar wind.

I tell you to be careful of the wind, as once it is released, no one can say where it will go or what it will do.

I heard it howling in my mind: **What have you done? What will you do now? You who are nobody, with nothing!**

Feeling unmoored from the old life felt frightening. But at the same time, I felt a strange exhilaration. That wind pushed me forward, whispering: **"You can do this. You can dream of a better life, a free life."**

I would love to finish my story right here and have you relieved, believing it was all easy and clean, that happiness *came right then and there.*

However, life is messy, with no straight road to follow. The road signs for *happiness-ever-after* aren't visible, especially when you need them the most. So, you must try to find your own way, and sometimes you must do so again and again.

Maybe I Didn't See Enough of Hell the First Time

After a few months without The Husband, the first sign of change appeared in my boys. Their father suddenly started buying them presents, something that had rarely happened in their lives. For me, these gifts were the harbinger of fresh hell.

I knew our current arrangement couldn't last forever, with the boys and me in the house, while The Husband lived with relatives. He had started practicing sobriety through AA, and in everyone's mind, the next logical step must have been reconciliation. Since he no longer drinks, shouldn't we make amends and become a couple again?

I saw the desperation mixed with hope in my sons' faces as they pleaded with me to let their dad come home. I felt myself turning back into stone.

Everything inside me screamed *no, no, no*. But I was too early into this freedom to trust myself. I hadn't yet found my voice and hadn't been free long enough. Just having The Husband nearby turned me into a frozen version of myself, someone I despised.

Yet, I painfully agreed to let him return.

What a mother will do for her children...

We were both trying.

However, watering ashes does not grow a marriage.

Deep inside, I knew it was not enough. Our lives seemed to have picked up where they had left off, the only difference being that he was sober. Nothing else had changed, and I could feel us all slipping back into our old patterns.

The crazy thing is, there was no talking.

There was no discussion about why I had wanted to leave him.

No discussion about how it had been for him.

No discussion about what he had done, or why he had stopped drinking, or why he had done all that drinking to begin with, and what about the drugs?

There was simply silence.

One evening, as he flicked a cigarette butt to the ground, he said offhandedly: ***"You know, the people at my AA meeting said I shouldn't tell you this, but I am. If I could have found you the day you left, I would have killed you."***[1]

He stared at me, his hazel eyes unwavering, while silence bloomed between us.

I didn't know what to say.

I certainly didn't know what to do; my body was frozen.

His words reverberated in my mind, shredding the fragile vision I had dared to build. The life I'd begun to dream of for my sons and myself vanished into a cloud of fear.

There's no prison more secure than the one we build for ourselves, and I had just locked the door by letting him back in.

We existed light years apart.

How could he think such a thing, say such a thing, and still believe we could have a marriage?

The only way I could make sense of it then was this: at least now I would know I had tried everything. I wanted to believe that giving him one last chance, now that he was sober, might change everything.

But we were doomed from the start.

His words echoed in my mind during the day and then again at night, keeping me awake. I lay in bed, terrified of the man sleeping beside me.

I didn't know him. Worse, I didn't want to.

There was no intimacy, and for that, I felt a sense of relief. He divided the bed in half with a rolled blanket and admonished me to stay on my side. No problem, I thought.

As he continued to attend his AA meetings, his behavior became increasingly bizarre. I had made two friends while he was gone, something new and challenging for me. There was one who had listened to me talk about my life. When she came to visit, he would glare at her until she left. Later, he complained to me that "He couldn't even enter his own kitchen because there were *people in the house.*"

Because there was one person ... talking to me.

I began to wonder if years of drinking and whatever drugs he had taken had cracked something deeper, something that couldn't be mended.

We tried marriage counseling one last time. This counselor was keen on exposing inappropriate behavior and called him out on his contradictions. My husband refused to return, accusing the counselor *he had chosen* of being biased against him.

Then came the demands.

He insisted that the boys and I attend Al-Anon meetings, claiming we couldn't heal as a family unless we did. The meetings didn't help, and he resented that we didn't participate in them more often.

The meetings traumatized the boys and did nothing to alleviate my fears. At that time, the discussions were not well facilitated. Attendees seemed to be trying to compete in whose drunk husband was the most violent and less about how to fix anything, more about how to survive inside the dysfunction.

To *survive* wasn't enough.

I wanted a different life without all the trauma.

That's when I realized something I never expected:

A sober alcoholic was worse than a drunk one.

It wasn't just the drinking that made us incompatible; it was the difference in our fundamental values and desires.

The same controlling, disagreeable behaviors remained, but sobriety gave them clarity, amplifying them. He now insisted we were the ones who needed fixing. He spoke to us as if we needed to be elevated. Elevated into what? I never knew.

Each day in our strained, silent existence felt heavier. We did nothing together. He ate alone in the bedroom or in front of the TV. He never asked me about my days, just as he never had before.

He would have had to be truly blind not to see that I had emotionally left long before I physically had. We were living like strangers under the same roof, two ghosts haunting the same shell of a house.

For years, he had made no connection with the boys and me. During his drinking, maybe he was too numb to notice or care. When he finally got sober, it was too late. He tried to resurrect something that had long burnt away. The damage had been done.

I never understood why counselors and support groups push so hard to save every marriage in the aftermath of addiction *or even during*. Sometimes, what is broken can't be rebuilt.

Sometimes, the miracle is not staying, it's in the leaving.

We remained strangers. I was still afraid to speak to him about anything. With my maid-like tendencies, I focused on the home and ensured that everything was done.

My health began to decline, which added to our problems. Several doctors had examined me while my husband's medical insurance still covered us. One doctor suspected a stroke, and another scheduled tests for a possible brain tumor. The medical appointments accumulated, with another doctor suspecting multiple sclerosis, but no clear answers emerged.

My body weakened, making it impossible to keep up with my responsibilities. Primarily, I still handled all tasks that needed to be done around the house. However, without my health, I struggled to balance my cleaning jobs with caring for my household.

Tasks piled up, and disorder settled in. Even though The Husband had stopped drinking and had been attending Alcoholics Anonymous meetings, He had merely swapped alcohol for meetings, spending most of his free time there.

One evening, he came home from work, set His keys on the dresser, and spoke in utter defeat:

"I can't do this anymore."

My mind scrambled for meaning. *Do what?*

"I can't be a father, a husband, work, and stay sober."

"I can't do this anymore," He added.

And that was that.

He wanted a marital separation and ordered me to sleep on the sofa from then on. He did not talk to me about his worries or the pain he was having, nor did he share with me anything that we could work on together. He did not elaborate on what we would do next, except to say that he planned to quit his job.

My income could never cover rent, all the bills, and feed us, and there was simply no way to clean any more houses than I was already doing.

But he had spoken the magic words!

Those words freed me from the church's marital obligations. I wanted to scream with relief, but at the same time, every tear I had ever swallowed poured out in my grief over our failures.

Each day, there was so little time left to change the future. Illness hampered everything I tried to do, leaving me too weary to focus. Days were like runaway trains, rushing us down the tracks and past the million things still undone.

To Save Us, I Had to Burn the Bridges

I didn't just walk away from our marriage and home; I made sure there was no way back. Because going back wasn't an option. It would be a return to silence, to fear, to watching my boys grow up learning all the wrong things about love. Perhaps people think "leaving" is the hard part, but the truth is, staying would have cost them more.

I branded myself the villain to buy them a better life story, even if it meant stepping into the fire myself. If anyone ever asked why I did it, I'll tell them this: *I chose to be the one who broke the cycle, not the one who passed it down.*

One night, in the middle of all this, I woke to the prickly feeling of being watched. Standing at the edge of the sofa, he loomed over me, staring down with hooded eyes. Hatred seemed to glitter behind them. I lay still, feigning sleep, terrified of what he might do next. At that moment, I knew. A separation would never be enough, not for him, not for us. My body flushed with fear, and I broke out in a cold sweat. What was behind his malevolent stare?

I couldn't find a lawyer fast enough. I needed him to never want me back. I felt terrified and driven to take this step.

So, I chose the one thing I knew he could never forgive. I planted a rumor—drawn from something I had read in the advice pages of his monthly *Playboy* magazine—something so grotesque to him he would never recover from it. It would stamp a blazing scarlet letter across my forehead.

He was obsessed with the idea that I would run away with another man, no matter what I said or did. It would be the death of me, of us.

I told this "Thing" to someone I knew would carry it, someone who thrived on passing things along. And she did not disappoint.

All I had thought about in that quick moment, in that impulsive decision, I could not get past the unsafe way he made me feel. Not allowing myself to sort out complications, not taking more time, I committed to the idea.

Later, when she learned we were separated, she called to tell me—since I didn't want him anymore, she did and planned to date him. I knew then the rumor had already taken root.

What I hadn't considered in my limited life experience and urgency to escape was how far it would spread. Rumors ripple like stones thrown into water. They don't stop where you intend. They reach your children, your family, your church. And once they reach your children, you can never call them back. I hadn't thought about how the indelible mark would remain on my forehead, a red letter branding me forever with everyone I had known. I was only thinking about making him go away.

At any cost.

You would think I was smarter than that, having learned from my first mistake in telling a secret in my youth and the damage it had caused. But in that precise moment, I didn't care. One question drowned out everything else in my mind: what kind of man wants to kill someone who doesn't want to be with them anymore?

There was no getting past that.

Later, when the rumor had become the best thing ever "in the chicken yard of the church," I felt myself waver on the very path I had set in motion. Because I knew exactly what I had done, I tried, in one weak moment, to hide it, even from myself. Admitting I had created it as a weapon, something to make sure he would never take me back, felt unbearable and frightening.

When he asked if it was true, I dodged the truth. But even the fear of thinking he might kill me did not change my mind because I knew this: **a man who could stand over me at night like that was not a man I could ever return to.**

What had I done? What kind of person had I become? And what would we do now?

The church had left me in this marriage and all these houses. My beliefs had kept me bound. Our families had abandoned us to our fate. So, if I had to be cast out to break free, I would walk out with the mark blazing.

The now Ex-Husband eventually quit his job and left us to go live with relatives again. I stood up from the ashes of our lives, wearing that mark on my forehead, relieved that it had bought my freedom, and all our freedoms, including his. *Yes, it was worth the price.* I never had to walk down that road and fall into that same hole again.

Hells End

When the divorce I paid for was formally in process, The Husband had gone to live in a different city with his parents, leaving the boys and me in the house. We couldn't continue living here, even with the money I earned, because the bills were more than I could afford.

There was no child support or alimony to be had.[2] This was how we lived for a short while.

One day, after I had cleaned two huge houses for over eight hours, I earned only $80 in cash. Back home, exhausted, I couldn't find the money anywhere! I was sure it had been in my pocket, my cleaning bucket, or the car, but despite tearing everything apart, I couldn't find it! I needed to get to the market, buy something to feed my kids, and put gas in the car, but it had simply vanished. We survived day to day then, and I felt myself break from the strain, the impossibility, the exhaustion, the wind that had blown us into this new life.

I dragged myself to the shower, desperate for a place to cry where the boys might not hear me. I tried to think of what I'd say to them, how I'd explain coming out with no money and no meal for the day. Once I started crying, the tears became heavy and endless. I wailed, crouching down with the shower water spraying loudly over me, hugging myself, grief rising from a deep, raw place that frightened me.

I regretted nothing about our freedom. I regretted the things I hadn't managed to finish, like college, or the decent wage-earning job that might have allowed me to take better care of the boys. At that moment, I was all they had and I knew deep inside it wasn't enough.

I felt The Husband and his family were waiting for me to fail, waiting for the day I'd have to turn my boys over to them, after all. It was my greatest fear as a mother.

A particular grief comes from being the only adult in a collapsing world. Knowing that if you fall, there is no one to catch you, and yet falling anyway, if only for a moment in the shower, where your children won't see. This is the sorrow I carried: The sorrow of having no one to rescue me.

One of my sons knocked softly on the bathroom door and asked if I was okay. Through sobs, I choked out that I'd lost all the money I'd earned. All I could think of was the hard work, my reddened hands, and broken heart. The boys huddled outside the door, and one asked gently how much I'd lost. Through tears, I wailed out, "All of it. Eighty dollars."

When I finally came out, they urged me to check the car again. I'd already looked many times, but they insisted, practically pushing me toward it. And there it lay—$80 crumpled on the floorboard in plain sight. It had not been there before. With the little bathroom window open, I suspected our neighbors (neighbors I'd never spoken to) might have overheard my cries and learned what had happened from the boys.

Maybe the money came from them, but my sons never revealed the truth. Too ashamed to ask, I stayed silent, lost in that mixture of survival and grief.

To this day, I don't know who placed the money there, or if I missed it because I was too exhausted to see clearly. But the moment taught me something: when we cry out, someone, seen or unseen, may be listening. Even in despair, mercy and grace sometimes slip through the cracks unnoticed, except by those whose lives depend on it.

Later, when everything collapsed entirely: my health, my jobs, and when the divorce was finalized, I fell into an economic decline worse than before. The boys and I moved into an illegal one-bedroom shanty shack down by the river—into a life I could have never imagined to be possible in America.

Grandma's yellow car, which she'd gifted me, died around that same time. It was creatively towed to our new "home," never to be revived. I simply never had the money to fix it. Its final trip became the one where it had valiantly tried to carry us far enough away.

For years, the five of us survived poverty together, wrapped in the isolating loneliness that public prejudice brings. Poverty is like social leprosy. It brought humility and the shame of never having enough, despite all the work I did.

But we were free.

And that freedom helped us embrace each new day.

There is nothing, *nothing,* like freedom.

We eventually had to leave this house and move again to another one.

Chapter Thirteen

House of Shack

At the Social Service Office

"What did you *do* that made your husband leave you?" the young social worker asked accusingly. My friend and I recoiled at her question. I felt like a teenager was interviewing me, clueless about life, unaware of her tone, and displaying a youthful lack of wisdom. Her judgmental expression and stiff posture made the hairs on the back of my neck bristle.

That moment marked the beginning of two years filled with prejudice, condemnation, and extreme poverty.

"I got sick," I replied after a long, stunned pause.

I had come to apply for what people commonly called welfare, officially known in California during the late 1990s as Aid to Families with Dependent Children (AFDC). After the 1996 Personal Responsibility and Work Opportunity Reconciliation Act (commonly referred to as welfare reform) was passed. AFDC transitioned into Temporary Assistance for Needy Families (TANF). California implemented this program as CalWORKs (California Work Opportunity and Responsibility to Kids).[1]

CalWORKs became the state's main welfare-to-work initiative, emphasizing employment while providing limited cash assistance to families in need.[2] It is limited to two years for your *entire life*.

My new friend, who had become an invaluable support, accompanied me to the social services office because welfare appeared to be my only option. The one-stop Job Services had sent me over to the Disability Office because of my apparent illness. I had trouble even holding a pencil, and a recent jogging injury left one leg longer than the other, causing a limp and difficulty with stairs. I no longer had medical coverage. They reviewed all my medical records, and deemed me severely disabled. I was encouraged to go to social aid and apply for college and welfare.

At first, I resisted the idea. I wanted a good job, but eventually, the truth stared me down: my illness was progressing. I had lost all my cleaning jobs; hopes and dreams alone couldn't pay rent or feed four sons. It seemed to be my only viable path.

The social service office felt cold and institutional, its bare gray walls adorned with posters detailing program rules and penalties for fraud. Comfort or warmth remained absent. Before meeting with the social worker, I was required to watch an orientation video about the welfare program in a room filled with other women, most noticeably younger than me. The movie left a bitter taste of despair and humiliation in my mouth.

Life isn't perfect, and safety nets exist for when things go wrong.

This net was laced with barbs.

How could I explain the disastrous train wreck of our lives to this young person, who seemed to have stepped straight from a college classroom into a desk job? She had no way of grasping the tangled years behind me: nearly 40, four kids, no job skills, and a husband who had forbidden college or career for most of my adult life. And then, when illness finally caught up with me, he had decided he wanted a separation.

What did she know of a difficult life and the mistakes that come with one?

I filed for divorce, understanding the separation served only as a tool for compliance. The Husband left, and we lost our home. He was not contributing financially, leaving his sons and me in the worst monetary situation we had endured yet. My illness was complex and challenging, but I had no time to indulge in being sick.

If I wanted this life of freedom, I had to fight for it with everything left in me.

During the interview, the worker shifted her tone slightly, after I mentioned my illness. She adopted a more businesslike manner. She said there had been a rise in men leaving their wives in my age group throughout the county. Maybe she meant it to make me feel less alone.

We did qualify for the social aid program, and state medical benefits, but the process was clearly designed to grind you down. Despite what some might believe, getting welfare isn't an easy ride. It was grueling and humiliating. I faced a gauntlet of requirements: monthly meetings, college coursework, 20 hours of work or job training per week, job-readiness classes, and endless paperwork. I still had to care for my sons, run our tiny home, and ensure they got to school without bus transportation in our new location. I had to drop my youngest off early, sometimes before dawn, because I had no other options.

My heart broke every time.

Thrown into this new life, I jumped over every hurdle and braced myself for the ones I couldn't. I desperately needed a better job to support my sons and secure a real home. Some days, the obstacles overwhelmed me, pushing me into corners of hopelessness. My pillow caught silent tears when the weight of it all became too much.

But I couldn't fall apart. My sons looked to me for their next meal, for stability and safety. Each day, I had to jump over new hurdles and run a race without a foreseeable finish line.

It takes a while to sort out the cost of freedom. Even with the cage door open, you still have to feed the children, find the keys to a new life, and outrun the shame others try to staple on your back.

Even in the darkest moments, synchronicity sometimes worked in our favor. Just as we had hit rock bottom, a small mercy arrived. My sons had made a friend at school whose grandmother owned property near the river. On that property stood what we came to call, *"The Shack."* Initially, the grandmother refused to rent it to us, fearing we would bring trouble. Somehow, her grandson convinced her otherwise, and I remain eternally grateful.

We had so little, but we had each other.

For now, that was enough.

The Shack

Welfare provided us with about $946 a month. The Shack cost $450. After paying essential bills, we ended up beyond broke. We also received around $175 in food stamps, which came in tear-out booklets resembling Monopoly money. The humiliation of having to use them made the boys reluctant to go shopping with me. With trembling fingers, I would tear out the correct amount at the checkout while the clerk and the customers watched.

On one of my third son's birthdays (which I now tried to celebrate), I bought a carton of ice cream and a bag of chips, such rare treats. A man behind me in the grocery store check-out scoffed loudly, "So this is what my tax dollars pay for? Junk food?"

My face burned with shame. At that point, I hadn't found my voice, never really having had the chance to use it, so I slunk out of the store, feeling everyone's eyes on my back.

Despite my best efforts, none of them knew how empty our pantry was or how we managed to salvage birthday celebrations from scraps. *That ice cream meant everything to my sons.*

People sometimes imagine survival looks like strength and courage. Still, sometimes it looks like silence, like slinking out of the grocery store with your head down, too tired to defend yourself, too heartbroken to speak, clutching the groceries your children waited all month for.

The Shack started out as a 32-foot silver bullet trailer. Someone had taken a chainsaw, cut off one side, and added a big, one-room extension. That extension was split into two spaces: a back room for the boys, a front room that served as my living space and the living room. I parked my bed right by the front door, determined to keep my kids safe. Each night, I slept with a knife under my pillow.

It was one thing to think you were free, and another to sleep with a knife under your pillow. Freedom, in those days, was just the absence of immediate threat, not the presence of peace and safety.

The trailer part of The Shack contained a small bathroom, a narrow closet area where I stored my belongings, and a tiny kitchen. It's messy to leave one life and start another, especially when you've never experienced living on your own. It was now up to me to build this new life from splinters and scraps. If there had been a self-help book for that, I wouldn't have had time to read it.

Despite the hardships, some people showed us kindness, and good things did happen.

One woman at the utility company went out of her way to help me close the old utility account, even though the rules didn't allow it, since the ex-Husband had opened it. The agency which rented that home to us was patient and kind with me, as I did my part by thoroughly cleaning the old house before leaving. Some of the things my husband abandoned still required attention but I left those for him to handle. Under California law, everything acquired together had to be divided equally, so I split the expensive dishes my mom had gifted us for our wedding: two plates for him and two for me. Their sentimental value had evaporated. The weight of things we once shared became too heavy to carry into freedom, so I took only what we needed.

The one friend who had stood by me through everything became my rock. She cheered me on as we fixed up The Shack and moved in. Embarrassment and nervousness had filled me at the thought of showing her the place, fearing she might say it remained unlivable. But the alternatives were worse. It was either low-income apartments riddled with drug activity or, as social services suggested, temporary housing tied to domestic violence cases, which only became available after losing our current home. *Then we would have to stand on a street corner with all the worldly goods we could hold—before they would help us.* That option terrified me.

I had never told anyone the full story of The Husband's treatment, not welfare, not counselors, not even my new friends. By that point in our journey, his abuse had mainly turned into neglect. I did not want more agencies to become involved. I only wanted safety and distance.

The Welfare system's rules made poverty feel even more degrading and brutal. Even my old, broken-down car counted as an asset, too valuable for eligibility, unless I downgraded to something older. The saving grace lay in its broken transmission, rendering it undrivable, so it didn't count against us.

We lived in a place most people would have laughed at, or pitied… a shack patched together with plywood, hope, and some duct tape. But inside lived four boys who still miraculously loved their mother, who refused to quit. Poverty humiliated us but it didn't break us. Freedom hurt but it didn't kill us. And in that strange little room where I slept with my knife, I began learning a hard truth: sometimes the lowest place isn't the end. *Sometimes it's the start of the climb.*

A Good Friend's Help and A Brother's Kindness

My younger brother eventually lent me an old car that met the requirements of the welfare program. Without that kindness, we could not "do life." We never spoke much, but his generosity saved us. Every place we needed to go was miles away.

I had stopped cleaning homes before going to social services because my health continued to worsen. Later, we discovered that some of my symptoms likely resulted from heavy-metal poisoning. The Husband had been making jewelry in our bedroom, using toxic materials with little to no ventilation, and neither of us had realized how harmful it had been.

When I cleaned out our last home, I remember scrubbing the bedroom walls with soapy water and watching the suds turn a deep, blood-red hue, like something out of a horror film. The rag, the water, even the walls themselves seemed to bleed beneath my hands. I stood there, staring at the streaks, realizing how much had seeped into those walls, into me, and how sick it may have made me.

This happened long before cell phones, so there was no quick way to snap a picture, or ask for help online. Lacking money for gloves and no one to call, I just kept scrubbing, dumping bucket after bucket of red water, determined to reclaim our cleaning deposit.

They used to say: What you don't know can't hurt you?

It's not true.

Determined to survive, I moved forward.

The Shack tested us in every way, and our attempts to fix it often turned into comedic misadventures. My friend's encouragement, the feeling that *someone* believed in me, made all the difference. When I finally built up the courage to show her the place, she walked in, looked around with her practiced contractor's wife eye, and said bravely, "It's OK. We can work with it; it's not so bad."

I am sure she kept her honest opinion to herself, but to me, she said, "We can do this!"

Her husband was a contractor, so she had learned some things about fixing homes, though maybe not like this. The Shack was a Frankenstein creation: part trailer, part lumber, part mystery architecture. There were gaps, broken windows, and a lot of cleaning needed.

It was a lot like an episode of "I Love Lucy" on TV, when we tried to paint the dark, dinghy wooden siding on all the walls. The paint slid down the boards in long, dramatic drools. We kept stepping into the paint pans, leaving footprints everywhere! It created a mess bigger than anyone could have imagined. Finally, my friend called her husband, who told her you were supposed to use *primer* first so that the paint would stick.

Primer? Who would have thought?

Their business had a lot of leftover paint from their contracting jobs, and with those supplies. My friend helped me transform the place with elbow grease, fresh paint, and salvaged carpet. With her help and encouragement, we converted The Shack into a livable space.

Incredibly small for five people, The Shack soon sheltered six. The boy whose grandma owned the property joined us informally. He had occasionally been sleeping in an abandoned car in a nearby field to escape the drug chaos at home. His parents were deeply entangled in drugs and dysfunction. Understanding his need for a safer environment, I offered him a place to stay, fully aware of what it meant to escape a life of dysfunction.

Daily dilemmas defined The Shack. The structure hadn't been sealed properly, and cold drafts entered through gaps where the trailer and the added wooden structure failed to align. The electricity came from a long, thick extension cord running through several oak trees and fields, limiting appliance use. If I toasted bread, I couldn't brew coffee at the same time. It was as illegal as they come, which is another reason the owner hesitated to rent it to us.

It had a questionable septic system, so we were careful.

It lacked a registered address, so I rented a P.O. Box.

And at night, creatures scurried across the roof. I'd pull the covers to my chin and stare wide-eyed at the ceiling, listening to the thumps, bumps, and frantic skittering above me. I imagined raccoons, but it was more likely that giant wood rats ruled the place. I set traps and tried everything to drive them out, but the rooftop remained their domain—a playground for the nightly roof-runners.

Encounters with people proved even more unsettling than those with animals. One field over, a strange man lived in an old cab-over trailer and often wandered around wearing only tighty-whitey underwear and a cowboy hat. He became a familiar figure to local neighbors and police. He was frequently taken away after wandering into people's homes, where he would be found sitting in their kitchens, eating their food. But, before long, he was returned to roam the neighborhood again, tipping his cowboy hat gallantly at me if we ever saw him.

As odd as he seemed, he didn't frighten me as much as the nighttime visitors who drove up the gravel road calling for someone named "Sonny." They would exit their car and yell his name and sometimes even approached The Shack.

My new fifth son loaned me his BB gun, which I kept by the front door. When these strangers appeared, I stepped outside, holding the BB gun visibly (never pointing it) and shaking the gun, I'd shout, "Sonny doesn't live here anymore!" my heart pounding in my chest.

Most of the time, they backed away quickly, raising their hands and muttering apologies before driving off.

I didn't want to be a threat.

I just didn't want to be prey.

Every woman who's ever lived alone knows the art of bluffing strength.

I later learned The Shack had once been a meth house, explaining much of its troubled history. Years after we moved away, I discovered that buildings used for meth production required hazmat-level cleanup, yet sadly, we had lived there unknowingly.

First Winter

Our first winter in The Shack was brutal. The wood stove provided very little heat at first. My limited firewood and lack of experience left me struggling to keep it burning effectively. I later learned how to use it, and it also became our oven since the trailer oven did not work. I could bake cornbread and put different things on top of the stove to heat.

Many aspects of the Shack life seemed unbearable. In moments of weakness, my anger simmered beneath the surface. For years, I had taken care of the Husband through his illness and drunkenness and lived under his rules. Now, feeling old, disabled, and solely responsible for four sons (and one extra), it felt as if we had been discarded without a second thought by all our families.

It was ridiculous to be angry. All I wanted was to be free. And I was, but freedom, as I was learning, had a price. Any loss presents stages of healing, and anger is one of them.

"I can't be a father, a husband, and take care of you, because I need to focus on staying sober," he had said.

He had found the bravery to end us, as he needed to save himself. And that was his reality, so how could I keep faulting him? At my end, wasn't I also busy trying to save the boys and myself? When I realized everyone had been doing the best they could, even if it wasn't enough, the anger eased its grip.

Despite these hardships, I felt a flicker of accomplishment. We had made The Shack livable. That meant we could survive for another day.

My friend taught me that even in the bleakest circumstances, kindness and faith in one another can spark hope.

It was a strange new feeling to have a friend, someone to talk to and do things with. I had a lot to learn about friendship after so many years spent in isolation. I hadn't had a serious one in years, and there were many social norms to understand. One time, she phoned me, mad and upset that I hadn't been calling her, even though she had been calling me all the time. It was an enlightening moment for me to realize that I could reach out. I didn't have to wait for her to call. Indeed, she needed me to call her as much as I needed her to contact me. My feelings of always being unwanted surfaced in these moments. Why would anyone want to listen to me talk about my life? Let alone choose to spend time with me?

Life at The Shack, of course, carried on. The drama seemed endless, with new dilemmas springing up daily. Maybe when my friend heard my stories, they were better than the soap operas on TV. And while I sometimes laughed at the absurdity of it all, the truth was that survival was no game show. Behind the laughter, The Shack held its own kind of menace. Safety was never guaranteed. I never knew what would happen from day to day, or what kind of trouble would land on my doorstep.

The boys' bedroom door, missing a doorknob, offered only a hint of privacy. Their single beds barely fit, and each kept his belongings in a large plastic tub. Five kids in one room brought its own storms, territorial flare-ups, clashing habits, and shifting alliances.

Fearful of intruders, I slept with one eye open, even after a kind acquaintance from church sent her husband to install a proper lock on The Shack's flimsy front door.

We had running water, though I never figured out its source or quality amidst the many other pressing concerns. A small five-gallon propane tank fueled cooking and warm showers but needed constant refilling. When desperation set in, help sometimes arrived without even being asked for. My friend or her husband would bring propane or invite us over for a meal. Those meals were islands of relief amidst the bareness of our cupboards.

We survived that first winter the way we survived everything— together, hungry for hope, and holding on by the thinnest threads of grace.

Broken Spirits

My spirit was already broken when I arrived at the social services office. I couldn't secure a job in my condition. My situation felt so hopeless. There's so much disdain for welfare moms in this country, even now. In the 1990s, we had become vilified and shamed, and when I became that statistic, I was no different. For two years, I relied on welfare and food stamps to survive, and society made sure I felt ashamed for it.

The public viewed people like me as burdens on society, lazy "takers," living off taxpayers' dollars. But the reality of welfare spending tells a very different story.

In fiscal year 1997, the United States federal government spent approximately $158.8 billion on all social welfare programs, including Medicaid, food stamps, SSI, and what people commonly referred to as "Welfare," representing about 9.9% of total federal expenditures.[3] Yet people acted as if it were bankrupting the nation. In truth, it costs less than $49 per American per month.

The needy became the new scapegoat. The public's anger wasn't directed at war budgets or corporate subsidies; it was aimed at welfare moms, the impoverished, sick, old, and disabled. In contrast, the government allocated approximately $293 billion for defense spending, roughly $90 per person per month, to fund the tools of war. It bears repeating: the public turned its wrath not toward war budgets but toward the sick, the poor, the old, and the disabled. They failed to see that behind every statistic stood a *real person* with a life, a family, and hopes for a better future.[4] They failed to see that a country is only as good as how it treats its most vulnerable populations.

During economic struggles, people often sought someone to blame. Welfare recipients, particularly single mothers, unfairly bore the blame for draining public resources. Politicians capitalized on this fear, framing welfare programs as burdens on "hardworking taxpayers" despite the tiny percentage of federal spending they consumed.

In the 1990s, despite no significant recession, welfare reform became a political priority. Leaders promised to reduce dependence on government aid, and programs like TANF (Temporary Assistance for Needy Families) pushed recipients into work, *even if those jobs paid unlivable wages, or, as in my case, you were disabled.*[5] The goal focused on cutting government spending and promoting "personal responsibility," ignoring the realities of single-parent households and poverty.

The infamous "welfare queen" myth, born in the 1980s, still lingers, painting single moms as lazy grifters. It was a lie, but with the help of politicians, it stuck. The system demanded we prove our worthiness in ways men never had to. Widows and the elderly were seen as "deserving." Single moms? Often not. They frequently fell into the "undeserving" category, as outdated moral judgments about family structure deemed them less worthy of assistance.

The stereotype, though false, persisted in the public imagination.[6] Women of color faced compounded discrimination. Welfare policies often carried an underlying racism, complicating their lives even more.

Despite it all, most of us, myself included, were doing everything we could to survive. The safety net was thin. It rarely lifted anyone out of poverty, but it kept us from drowning for a while.

Welfare moms didn't crash the economy.

We didn't start wars or hoard billions.

We weren't bankrupting America from our Shacks.

But we were easy to find and easy to shame.

Hardships Pile Up

One of the worst social aid program meetings I attended featured a balding, overweight man in a sweat-stained suit standing at the front of the classroom. About ten other girls sat with me, all much younger than I was.

He seemed to despise us and made it clear, *"If you have family or friends elsewhere, leave this county. We don't want welfare moms here,"* he said derisively. *"Whatever you did to get into this position isn't our problem. Don't expect us to bail you out."*

Today, I would have recorded his words on my phone and possibly exposed his cruelty. Back then, I had no way to document what was said to us there.

As he ridiculed each of us, he sneered when he got to me, pointing at my fingernails. *"No job will hire you with those fingernails,"* he scoffed.

We were encouraged to look professional at one of the training classes, told to pay attention to our clothes and appearance. Makeup wasn't allowed in our church and learning how to wear it was a curveball for me. It was a cheap polish at $0.99 per bottle, an extravagant purchase at the time. Moreover, because I couldn't decide which color I liked, I had painted each finger a different color. Five bright, beautiful hues that, as an artist, greatly appealed to me. I had spent five dollars on myself. I didn't know it would be a hurdle for employment, or another excuse for someone to shame me.

I realized what he said was inappropriate and demoralizing, but we all sat frozen and silent. He was there to scold us for our "bad life choices," pointing out some perceived flaws in each of us as if humiliation were part of the job training. He even gave us a written test designed to embarrass us.

It only fueled my resolve. I remember thinking, *I'll take your job someday and do it better than you.* That never happened, of course. Life had other plans, but I hope today's women keep their phones charged and ready.

Life led me down a winding path with no time to dream. We were cattle, prodded and pushed through chutes, headed towards someone else's idea of a goal. Plenty of nights, I cried. Life in that Shack tested us in ways that felt impossible.

It was hard, and I cannot say that enough.

It was difficult to believe I was living in America with the hardship and lack that swallowed us whole.

My sons wanted normal, everyday lives like those of their classmates, but that wasn't happening. They never once asked for their dad to return, and they barely spoke of him, at least as far as I knew. I wondered if they felt abandoned…or relieved.

The boys were not inclined to complain much to me about our circumstances, even though there was plenty of fodder for it. Not a day went by without some struggle or problem. They became master problem-solvers, creative in so many ways, trying to meet their needs with what we had at our fingertips. They were lonely for friends, but social prejudice lay over us like a shadow. It's hard to attract friends in thrift-store clothes and duct-taped shoes.

When one of them wanted to invite a friend from school over, I instinctively knew this could be a bad idea. Sure enough, when the boy's mother pulled up and scanned our home, she refused to let her son out of the car. They just stared at our house. She rolled her window down. "No, this isn't happening," she snapped, adding a few more sharp words before driving off.

Didn't she realize she was only a paycheck or two away from being me? My sons never invited new friends over again.

Poverty isn't just hunger and cold. It's watching your children learn too early who the world thinks is worthy, and realizing you'll spend years teaching them a different truth.

When Even Pencils Are a Luxury

Sometimes, finding school supplies seemed impossible. One of my sons avoided telling me about the daily "F" he received because he had lost his only pencil, and someone had stolen his paper binder. He needed a nickel to buy a pencil from the teacher but we didn't even have that. None of the students would lend him one, and they all just stared while the teacher berated him. When he finally told me, my heart broke. The humiliation he endured weighed on me heavily. I hated those moments and felt like a failure as a mother.

At that time, I couldn't afford gym clothes for all my sons, who attended junior high and high school together. In truth, I had thought any t-shirt and shorts would suffice. Without telling me, they accepted an "F" every day in P.E. because they couldn't dress down. The school did not call until nearly report card time, by which time the damage had already been done. Once again, I didn't know what I didn't know, and had no mom friends to tell me otherwise. And just like many other teens, the papers sent home for parents didn't find their way to me. It seemed the school had no compassion, only criticism, perhaps finding it hard to believe that I didn't have a nickel. When I admitted our poverty at the teacher-parent meeting, they gave the boys lost-and-found gym clothes, uncaring of whether they fit or not.

I wished I'd had a spark of Mrs. Johnson's *Harper Valley PTA* fire, the kind that stands up to judgment, but I didn't know about her then.[7] I could only put out so many fires in our lives, and the ones I couldn't reach simply burned on. So many things slipped through my fingers as

I struggled to meet the county's demands. I no longer wondered why children in poverty received such poor grades. It wasn't because they lacked intelligence. It was because of deprivation and all the invisible battles. My sons never told me about many of their hardships, and that is another kind of heartbreak.

My children qualified for free lunch, but to receive it they had to stand in the "poverty line" while the rest of the students queued in the line of privilege. More often than not, my sons chose to skip lunch rather than endure teasing for being poor. Shame outweighed hunger.

Meanwhile, our car seemed to break down constantly. Soon, every tow truck driver in the county knew where The Shack was. One of my sons attended an auto shop class, and another had a natural talent for fixing things. Once, together, they strapped a box fan into the car's engine to keep it cool after the radiator fan failed. It got us through. At college, the auto shop teacher had his students fix my car several times. I paid for parts, and they learned about real car problems.

As societal slights piled up and my children realized others saw them as "white trash," some of them entered dark periods where they no longer wanted to live. We had gone from looking like a church-going, put-together family, to outcasts of society who didn't even have pencils at the ready. I understood their pain. At an age when they should have been stepping into the world with confidence, supported by a stable home, they found themselves at the bottom of the barrel, staring up at its slippery walls.

I remained trapped in the exhausting cycle of meeting the state's requirements to receive the small amount of money that barely kept us afloat. I had done this to all of us, albeit at my children's request, but I had put us here.

Nothing compared to the pain of seeing a child so overwhelmed by hopelessness that death seemed preferable. That burden nearly broke me. I had kissed their tiny toes as babies, whispered love into their ears, but they didn't feel that now. I always held onto some hope.

They had none.

In all the terrible experiences I had endured, I had never truly wanted to die; to escape from the sadness and pain perhaps, but never for death itself. Indeed, I thought about what dying might be like once or twice, but the worry of what would happen to my sons kept me trying to believe there could be better days ahead. My sons, however, had no such vision. They only knew the pain of going without, of a mother too harried and busy, and an unengaged, alcoholic father who had disappeared.

This was our life.

For months, I lived in terror of a phone call at work, or the moment I might walk into our home to find one of them hanging from the porch rafters, or some other unimaginable scene. The fear consumed me. A small part of me even felt cheated out of my own breakdown; I had no time for one. My sole purpose was to keep them alive and tethered to the world.

Of course, we attended counseling. Some state agencies attempted to help, but never truly understood our reality. We operated in a world where assistance programs came with fine print and endless paperwork, where food stamps resembled Monopoly money, where schools failed to notice children struggling in silence, kids so poor they couldn't even buy a pencil.

Somewhere along the line, I started forgetting how to get to wherever I was going when driving. I'd pull over in a panic, heart pounding, sweating, and totally confused—unable to remember the way to work, college, or home. After calming down, I would get back on the road and go bit-by-bit until I eventually reached my destination.

Maybe I was losing my mind? I had a hard time remembering people, places, and things that should have been ingrained in my memory. My brain was like a broken file cabinet, papers spilling everywhere. Think of the movie, *50 First Dates* with Adam Sandler and Drew Barrymore, where every day is a new day for the main character. I felt a bit like her, and still have some of these same symptoms, complicating my life today.

Poverty didn't just take *things* from us; it chipped away at dignity, choice, confidence, and the quiet sense that your life matters. I kept going, even when I feared my sons might not. A mother's love can be fierce, but in those years, it had to be a shield, a lantern, and sometimes a life raft.

River Secrets and Sacred Soil

My oldest son made a friend who dared to visit. He lived one field over. When he came inside for the first time, he drank nearly half a gallon of milk straight from the jug while my sons watched, horrified but too polite to stop him. That milk was supposed to last the week. Then, he asked if we had juice, chips, or soda. My sons just stared. Wasn't it evident from our home that luxuries like that were out of reach? That boy had likely never experienced actual financial limitations, always having whatever he needed at his fingertips.

Determined to change our situation, I carved out a small garden in the corner of a field that had once been a pigpen. The fencing remained intact, making it a perfect space.

Once we started harvesting, hunger no longer loomed over us. There was always a vegetable, a potato, a bean, or a squash to eat. It might not have been what they wanted, but it beat the dry, out-of-date, sometimes spoiling, weird food bank donations we had relied on before. I sometimes worked in the garden at night with a headlamp, since my days were full.

One summer, I secured a job at the same school my children had once attended. I worked as an administrative assistant in the principal's office. I could hardly believe I was sitting at a desk at the very school that had been so difficult to navigate in our poverty. The principal at the time said she did not hire me for my skills but because I was kind and knew how to help people, even stressed-out, angry people. *It was the one skill my husband inadvertently taught me.* Other skills I would pick up over time.

By the time I left that job, the school had better ways of helping students from economically challenged homes. There is now a clothing and supply room where students can get what they need. The lunch line was changed so no one would know who was paying for lunch and who was on lunch aide. These things help take some of the sting out of poverty for students.

That job was a massive stretch for me, having never held a "real" job before. I knew nothing about running an office, but I jumped in with both feet, grateful and happy to be working.

I would put on my ratty old clothes before daylight, go down to the river, and fish to feed my sons at night. I knew just where to go in the river and what bait to use. I would toss the fish into the sink without finishing the scaling, quickly scrub my hands, put on my work clothes, and head to my school job. No one at the school ever knew that the secretary behind the desk, in her modest skirt and heeled shoes, had just caught her family's dinner at the river.

Since we didn't have money and couldn't go to many other places, going to the river nearby became our solace. We spent many evenings and weekends appreciating the beauty of our surroundings, swimming in the cool water, grateful that it flowed past, taking our pain and sorrows with it.

So many experiences, both tragic and joyful, shaped our time at The Shack. For example, one winter, when the boys found a car hood, they piled onto it and slid down the hill on the snow that glistened in our field. Once home from school, they were stuck on the property, running around like Peter Pan boys and doing whatever boys do in the woods, making their own fun. I tried to console myself, grateful that at least they were not at the drug apartments.

Some memories have faded, while others remain etched in my mind. Strangely, the sons who most seemed to hate those years now tell me they were some of the best times of their lives. They say those hardships forged them into stronger people, better equipped for life than many of their peers. They learned that when you have nothing left to lose, you discover just how much you can achieve.

We lived at The Shack for years. One-by-one, as my sons reached high school graduation, they left to forge their own paths. I hadn't found a better-paying job fast enough to lift us out of poverty, nor ease their entry into adulthood, but they each found a way. Eventually, they would carve out their lives with grit, heart, and resilience.

The Big Wide World Full of People and New Ideas

I met some very kind people along the way, as well as some disagreeable ones, but I remained excited to be in this big, wide world full of opportunities, hoping to carve out a niche for myself and my boys.

One of the ladies I met was a military captain with a daughter who had special needs. Since my friend was stationed overseas, she asked me to help balance her daughter's checkbook. The catch: we had to meet at a local bar/dance club on Thursday nights, the only night with a no-alcohol, no-drug policy. I was terrified. I had never gone into a bar alone. But Thursday night turned out to be the perfect choice. It brimmed with people in recovery, some of the kindest, most open-hearted souls I'd ever encountered.

I helped her balance the checkbook, and in return, she taught me hip-hop. It was a whole new experience, joyful and freeing! Sometimes, healing doesn't come from therapy but from learning to laugh in a room full of strangers who have also survived something. That night, hip-hop wasn't just a dance; it was a reminder that my body still remembered joy.

One such night, I noticed a man who caught my attention. He wasn't like other men I had seen there. I watched him move around the room, dancing with various women, including one who was using a walker. His kindness impressed me. When he asked me to dance, I said no. The ladies had pre-warned me: once you dance with a man, you can't get rid of him. And the last thing I wanted was another man. But we saw each other there every Thursday night, sharing glances across the dance floor.

Later, I learned he was there to meet his friend, the DJ, who was spinning great tunes. He had a daughter and worked in the olive oil industry. He learned I was divorced and had five boys, a revelation I used to keep men away.

Meanwhile, I had reached the two-year limit of the welfare program and graduated from college with honors, earning an Associate of Science degree. I even received a scholarship, though I never got to use it. I was the first woman in our family's line to attend college and earn a degree.

Life still resembled a runaway train, with me desperately clinging on as it swerved wildly down the tracks. There just wasn't enough time and energy, and the thought of returning to school for two more years seemed impossible with my new full-time job.

When I called my social worker to inform her of my new job at a local high school, she congratulated me with sarcasm before delivering bad news: welfare claimed they had overpaid me and demanded repayment. Enraged, I thought of all the hoops I jumped through for barely enough to live on. My new job paid just over $9 an hour, nowhere near enough to escape poverty, and their repayment demands would have left me homeless. They hadn't even hired competent workers to calculate benefits correctly! How could that happen?

I sought legal help. A low-income lawyer swiftly dismissed their claim, revealing that our county often tried to recoup funds from recipients once they became employed.

Meanwhile, my ex-husband owed both child support and repayment for the state assistance I had received. Years passed before any child support arrived. By then, the boys were grown and long gone. When The Husband eventually applied for disability, I began receiving $50 a month. I deposited that money into an account with a special debit card for my boys, which my mother managed, allowing it to accumulate as needed.

If I didn't want The Husband, I didn't want his money either.

Much later, the county courts pressured me to forfeit my right to child support so they could pursue my ex-husband for their state reimbursement (And I thought, *Why does the public despise welfare recipients if it's being paid back?*) If he failed to pay, they would jail him. I found it ironic that in all those years I had raised my sons alone, they had never pursued him for support. But once he re-entered the system to sign up for SSI, they prioritized their money over my son's needs. By accepting the child support, I kept him out of jail because the entire bill had to be paid first before the county could recoup its money.

My boys had moved forward, flying out into the world like birds from a nest. They built their futures with creativity and courage, finding lives I never could have imagined for them. I stayed behind in The Shack, unable to afford better housing, despite working full-time.

Very few people knew how I lived or the daily challenges I faced. Making new friends at my age felt impossible, especially with an illegal Shack as my home and years of isolation. Yet, despite it all, freedom filled me with joy.

The pain, the struggle, it had all been worth it.

I had been so afraid to leave the familiar, even the terrible familiar. I learned that the unknown isn't always filled with monsters. Sometimes, it holds the life you've been dreaming of all along.

I no longer felt anger towards my ex-husband. If anything, I hoped he found happiness, maybe even a partner better suited to him. Anger, grief, and sorrow faded when I stopped feeding them.

I came to understand that these emotions couldn't fix the past or create a better future. Forgiving him, forgiving myself, and hoping our children would forgive us *both* for our mistakes became my greatest wish.

Without the chaos of that failing relationship, I had silence and stillness. In that quiet, I could think, breathe, find compassion for our younger, more ignorant selves, and feel grateful for second chances. Every day became an opportunity. My life belonged to me now, and I refused to carry the burdens of the past on my back.

Somewhere along the way, I came to understand that kindness is not just a suspicious transaction from manipulative people. I value true kindness, and believe it's a reflection of who you are, not what you get in return. You can't always control what you get in life, but you can choose to be truly kind.

Did I Give Up On God?

Not entirely. I believe in some sort of higher intelligence, but not in religion as it's presented in this world. Too often, it seems to exist on power, control, fear, and lies.

I still love having someone to thank for life's goodness, someone to listen to my sorrows in prayer. But my evolving beliefs no longer rule my life with fear and control.

Grace, though — *that* I do believe in.

Grace is the invisible thread that catches us when everything else falls apart.

I define it as that unearned gift of love. My belief stems from action, not because churches say so, but because I saw it in how my boys forgave my failings; in a friend who said, "We can work with this;" and in the gifts of dinner and propane when we had none.

I felt it after eighty dollars had shown up when the cupboards were bare. I felt it from a birthday card that one friend from high school sent me every year. I saw it in the tow truck driver who didn't charge me after seeing The Shack. I saw it in the college instructor who had his students repair my car for only the cost of parts. I saw it in every single act of kindness that strangers and friends had given me.

That's where I found my sort of God again, in the quiet places where no one but Grace was looking.

I eventually had to leave this house and move again to another one.

"The moment we choose to love, we begin to move against domination, against oppression."

~ bell hooks

Chapter Fourteen

The Olive Man

Remember the man I mentioned at the dance hall? When my sons and I were still living in our Shack home, I'd catch glimpses of him here and there about town. Once, I spotted him at the farmers' market selling olive oil. I nudged my friend and whispered, "That's the Olive Man!"

I had been telling her about him for weeks.

"He has adorable legs," she said with a smile.

"I know," I agreed.

One of the most complex parts of surviving a bad relationship is realizing that you risk walking into another one, unless you've done the healing work.

It takes time to trust yourself again after leaving someone who taught you to doubt your instincts and intuition. Healing isn't about just obtaining freedom. It's about learning what love is, what it isn't, and what it should never cost. It takes time to regain trust in yourself. Traumatized people will often seek out the familiar, even if it is a terrible thing to be with.

That truth weighed heavily on me. I had five teenage boys back then to care for, and the last thing they wanted in their lives was another man. I had seen too many single mothers bring home strangers, forcing their children into uncomfortable situations. I refused to do that to my sons.

If a man approached me in public, all five boys would suddenly appear, standing around me like a protective wall. Their silent presence sent men fleeing, and I always told them, "Good job, boys!"

Eventually, I agreed to meet the Olive Man in town for a meal. He nearly choked on an eggplant sandwich when I mentioned I'd been married for over 18 years. I was surprised to learn that he was older than me, and his daughter was turning seven. Careful not to be in anyone's debt, I paid for my own meal.

We started meeting occasionally but I refused to share my phone number or address. I didn't want a man in my home. That rule stayed firm for a long time, so deep ran my fear of falling into another trap.

Instead, I gave him my P.O. Box and told him he could write me letters. Soon, my stack of letters grew. Through them, I learned about his incredible life adventures, so different from mine. His handwriting scrolled across the paper, beautiful and deliberate, filling page after page. Sometimes, he wrote poetry. At other times, he shared profound thoughts. It came as no surprise that I found myself falling in love with him. I had never known a man who spoke about such fascinating things or who showed such a genuine interest in me.

The dilemma of introducing him to my five boys, and the place I lived in, weighed heavily on me. I decided to take him catfishing with my youngest son; night fishing beneath a full moon seemed like just the right kind of test. I don't recall if we caught fish but I know he won my son's heart. If that son thought he was okay, maybe the rest would, too.

The Talisman

I wanted my boys to feel like they had a say in what happened in our lives. So, I created a talisman: a small bag crafted from deer hide and attached to a leather neck strap. I told each boy to place something inside that represented them. One son, an electronics whiz, tucked a tiny transistor in. Each added something meaningful. I added a tiny lock of my hair.

Then I explained the rule: *if this man ever came to our house without this talisman, you get to decide if he stays to visit, not me.*

I wanted them to know they had power.

The Olive Man took it seriously, treating it as a solemn agreement. Whenever he visited, the boys stood guard at the door, asking him to show the talisman entrance fee.

One day, he arrived with grocery bags full of food, ready to cook a meal for my sons. A full BBQ spread: chicken, mashed potatoes, and all the fixings. A luxury we hadn't had in such a long time. He won them over instantly. Young at heart, he jumped right in, playing Magic cards with them and spending time with them in a way their actual father never had.

From then on, when his loud, clunky truck rumbled down the valley toward the river, the boys would chant "BBQ! BBQ!" jumping up and down and shaking The Shack floor with excitement.

He learned they had never really gone anywhere with me unless it involved a church function or a visit to their aunt. There had been no camping, no real adventures with me, no time, no money. So, he rented a van and took us all to the desert. We had all been holding our breath, half-certain the trip would vanish like all their father's old promises. But when that van pulled up, and we all piled in, we realized it was real.

Around the campfire, he shared stories of his adventures, sparking their imaginations. He made adventures seem possible, effortless, even ordinary, as if this was how life was meant to be lived. He had deep roots in the organic food industry, gifting us with boxes of wonderful food, bags of staples, even truckloads of firewood, and giving us a better life than we had been living for a long time.

During my last term of college, while he was a temporary landscape worker there, I'd find the letters **S** and **B** arranged in a heart shape of tiny white stones in the flower beds along the path to my class. When we decided to deepen our relationship, he scattered rose petals all along the walkway to his house as an invitation.

A romantic move, hard to resist.

I met his little daughter, and she became a dream come true. Surrounded by sons, I had once longed for a daughter, and there she was, just the kind I had imagined, the perfect mix of tomboy and lady. I shared my old dolls with her and read her stories. Though I didn't get to spend as much time with her as I'd have liked, for a little while, I had a daughter to love. She split her time between her dad and her mother's family, enjoying all the sports and adventures that childhood had to offer.

Then, one day, the Olive man showed up at our door without the talisman. A few of the boys ran up to me, eyes wide, faces worried.

"He doesn't have the bag!" they whispered loudly.

I shrugged. "It's your decision."

I wanted them to understand the talisman wasn't a pretend thing; that their power was absolute.

"Wait—wait!" the Olive Man cried, realizing they might close the door. "I have something!"

He sprinted back out to his car and returned carrying a whole case of expensive, high-end root beer, which he presented to the boys standing guard.

"If I give you this, can I come in?" he bargained.

They grabbed the root beer, grinning from ear to ear.

The door opened.

The talisman had done its job.

I happily blame him for inspiring my boys to dream. A couple took up crab fishing in Alaska. Another became an honored military guard. One bought land in the outback of Oregon and created an off-grid home with earthbags. My youngest built a replica of the famous Doctor Who's phone booth, the TARDIS, as the doorway into his underground home. The fifth son became a computer whiz, rising from the ashes of his family history to forge excellence.

Olive Man and I dated for seven more years before we married. It took that long for me to be certain, and for our lives to settle into a shared path. The world rushes single people into relationships again, as if we can't be whole on our own. But taking the time to heal was the bravest thing I've ever done. And let me say healing isn't a destination. It is a long journey, happening every moment of every day for me.

I am so grateful I gave myself time, time to be alone, to study, to heal, and to understand why I had once been lost in dysfunction. I am working on finding my voice and learning what a healthy relationship really means.

I allowed myself to love again.

Of all my hardships, the saddest would have been not finding love or never genuinely living in the freedom I struggled for.

I moved into a new house, and we made it a real home.

"Recovery can take place only within the context of relationships; it cannot occur in isolation."

~ Judith Herman, *Trauma and Recovery* 1992

Chapter Fifteen

The House of After

The new house came with an automatic garage door, a spacious outdoor porch, and windows overlooking the surrounding oak forest. I went from living in a literal shack down by the river to a clean, new, one-room studio home that was already stretched to capacity with Olive Man, myself, and his daughter part-time. They had been living there before I came along, and I was stepping into a life already in motion.

It was a far distance from town and my work, but once there, the privacy and the grounds made up for the extra travel. Olive Man had planted a large garden and fruit trees and maintained an in-ground pool and pond for the landowner, whose mansion sat at the top of the property like a quiet overseer. The land felt tended and intentional, a sharp contrast to the instability I had come from.

The change was so dramatic that, at first, the place felt like a motel—a temporary stop before I would have to move on again. For a long time, I felt like a trespasser. He was middle-aged like me, which meant we each arrived with our own toaster, our own bed, and our own sofa. We both had belongings and histories and blending them into a one-room home required more letting go and acceptance than I had anticipated.

His job as the property manager involved paying rent by maintaining the grounds, so after finishing my own full-time job, I joined him whenever I could. I helped with weed-whipping, pool cleaning, and housework up at the mansion, feeling a constant need to contribute, to earn my place, to prove I was not a burden.

The Olive Man had never had very long relationships and had never married. His daughter found the transition challenging. After having her father and their home entirely to herself, it was only natural that my moving in brought up prickly feelings and growing pains for all of us. I understood her resistance even as I struggled to navigate it.

When things finally smoothed out and this new life offered a sense of safety, new challenges still cropped up. I had never raised a daughter before, and after years of only boys, I often doubted whether I was doing anything right. My children were off living their own lives, and now each of us—Olive Man, his daughter, and I—had our own steep learning curve to climb before harmony could begin to take shape.

The strange life I had lived before did not prepare me for real life or for healthy relationships. Even though I had escaped my oppressive past, I had no template for how to live in freedom. The Olive Man was the most extreme example of the opposite of oppression. He had a gentle, old-hippie, "live and let live" approach to life, while I was recovering from a severe case of Church Lady Syndrome.

He never told me what to do or set boundaries around where I could go or whom I could see. He didn't take money from me, regulate my clothing, or isolate me from friends. His refrigerator held more food than we could ever eat, and he asked me what I wanted in nearly every situation. All of it was so foreign, so unfamiliar, that it made me anxious. I worried constantly about my inability to answer the simplest question: *What do you want?*

I had stopped wanting years earlier. I had stopped even thinking about what I might want from life. I could see that this frustrated him, but I didn't know how to fix it. I began compiling a list of things I knew I *didn't* want but creating a list of what I *did* want felt impossibly harder.

His life experience had given him a worldview that the world was mostly good, filled with more joy than problems. My experience had taught me the opposite: that the world was dangerous, unpredictable, and something to endure rather than enjoy. Those opposing views clashed often, and learning to understand one another would take time.

He was always ready for adventure, treating home like a waypoint between experiences. At first, I shared that eagerness, until the reality of a full-time job, property responsibilities, and household chores began to pile up. The excitement gave way to exhaustion.

The stress of my former life, combined with new severe job-related injuries, began to take a toll on my health again. At the time, I didn't understand how deeply living in trauma, oppression, and fear could wreak havoc on the body, compounding every new ache and illness that came along.

Years later, in counseling, I learned that living in fear doesn't just wound the heart, it rewires the brain. The part meant to calm me down had weakened, while the part that screamed danger had grown louder and louder. Memories from the past refused to stay there, leaking into the present as if the harm were still happening. I learned there was a name for this: trauma's fingerprint on the brain, invisible from the outside, but reshaping everything within.[1]

I began to worry that Olive Man had partnered up with a lemon—damaged goods. I feared he would grow tired of the constant ailments and caretaking. More than once, I considered leaving, convincing myself it would be kinder to him. In my darkest moments, I saw myself as a millstone around his neck. I carried that belief in secret sorrow, along with the quiet ache that I might never be good enough.

Then the devil in the details raised its horned head. I was still trying to maintain my old religious standards, keeping the house ready for Christ's return, the only role and purpose I had ever known, *even after that belief had collapsed into ash.* The imagined judgment of others weighed heavily on me, especially when it came to his friends, as I had but one of my own. Our standards for what mattered were vastly different, and reconciling them felt impossible.

The work felt endless. There was always more to do, even beyond my paid job. And yet, amid the exhaustion, I began collecting dreams I had never allowed myself before: pigeons, goats, chickens, and more gardening. Each dream felt like fulfillment and impossibility all at once, carrying with it even more work and responsibility.

Olive Man struggled to understand why I was the way I was. He had grown up with a *Brady Bunch* childhood: a loving family, countless adventures, and friendships still intact decades later. I carried a secret, shame-soaked past and a lifetime of beliefs that no longer fit the world I lived in.

I had trouble understanding how the people I lived with didn't instinctively know where the laundry basket was, where dirty dishes belonged, or that messes could be cleaned without my intervention. Order mattered to me. Cleanliness gave me a sense of creativity and purpose. I worked harder on things that felt invisible to everyone else, and resentment quietly took root.

On the surface, I had everything I never knew existed for me: a quiet place, a kind man, and a daughter I had always wanted. My sons were thriving in their own lives. The garden overflowed with food, herbs, and fruit, ready for harvest. Olive Man took me on adventures to places I never knew existed, showing me parts of the world I had never seen.

He once drove me all the way to the desert for a date shake he promised would be ecstatic—and it was. Through him, I gained access to a network of friends and family, to movies, theater, music festivals, traditions, and mutual care. Yet inside, I still carried the weight of where I had come from.

I didn't know how to accept kindness. I could say "thank you," even smile, but it felt foreign, like speaking a language I had never learned. Every gift came with invisible strings in my mind. Every kind act felt temporary, conditional, and fragile, as though it could be taken away at any moment.

People spoke easily of adventures, comfort, and laughter, sharing their lives in unguarded company. I believed those things belonged to some other world—a world that came with instructions I had never been given. I didn't believe they were real, not for someone who felt as broken as I did. Ease and joy seemed reserved for people who had done life correctly, people who hadn't made the mistakes I carried.

That belief lasted until I learned something crucial: I wasn't broken. I was un-tooled. I had entered adulthood without the basic instruments needed to navigate safety, choice, and belonging. Tools, I realized, could be gathered. Tools could be learned. That understanding shifted how I saw myself—not defective, but unfinished, still capable of growth.

So, when I stepped into a life with gardens, grocery lists, and a man who called me his love, I didn't feel settled or secure. I felt like a visitor, still listening for the next slammed door, still braced for the moment I would be told I didn't belong.

I kept waiting for someone to pull back the curtain and say, "You don't belong here." For a long time, belonging had never meant comfort. It had meant survival and silence, reading moods before words were spoken. That kind of training doesn't vanish just because you step into a safer place.

I didn't move easily through that new life. Inside, I was like a skittery cat, alert to every sound, watching constantly for the next shoe to drop. I looked for dropped shoes everywhere, scanning for danger even when none was visible. The absence of chaos felt wrong. Where was the drama, the conflict, the eggshell moments that had once dictated my every move? Fitting into what everyone else called normal felt like wearing clothes sewn for someone else's body, close enough to function, but never quite right.

I could sit in a room full of friendly people and still feel like a shadow, smiling and nodding while silently studying the script. Choice was the hardest skill to learn. When you've lived without it, even small decisions feel loaded with consequence. Choosing wrong had once come with punishment, ridicule, or silence. Choosing at all felt dangerous. I learned to hesitate, to defer, to say, "Whatever you want is fine," even when it wasn't. That habit followed me into my new life like an unwanted shadow.

Even simple questions—like "What would you like to drink?"—could make me freeze. In my earlier life, no one had ever asked a question in a way that implied real choice. Wanting something openly had never been safe. I had learned that preferences could provoke anger or disappointment, so I learned to erase them. Questions about weekends or the past carried the same weight. Social gatherings left me exhausted, overwhelmed, and hyper-aware, as if I had run a race no one else knew had started.

What surprised me most was how exhausting peace could be. Without a constant crisis to manage, I had to learn how to rest, how to sit still, how to exist without scanning the room. Calm exposed how tired I truly was. Some evenings I would retreat early, not because anything was wrong, but because everything was unfamiliar. Safety required a different kind of stamina.

I had to practice wanting things. Not big things at first, just preferences. Tea instead of coffee. Sitting by the window. Saying no without explaining myself. Each choice was a tiny act of rebellion against a past that had trained me to disappear. Over time, those choices began to stack, creating something sturdier than fear: a sense of self that could be trusted.

Counseling didn't erase my past, but it gave me language for it. Words I had never known existed suddenly explained reactions I had blamed myself for. Trauma, hypervigilance, conditioning—these weren't moral failures; they were adaptations. Understanding that loosened something tight inside me. I wasn't weak for struggling. I had been strong for surviving.

Books helped too. I underlined passages, folded corners, and returned to sentences that felt like permission slips. Each insight became another tool in my growing kit. Slowly, I stopped judging myself for needing help. Needing help, I learned, was not the opposite of independence. It was evidence of healing.

Slowly, I had to learn how to accept kind words without suspicion, how to stand still when someone hugged me, how to believe that a smile might be genuine. I learned I could cook in a quiet kitchen without punishment for burning a dish—or for not cooking at all. Freedom doesn't feel like freedom at first. For me, it felt dangerous. But when someone is patient enough to stand beside you, and you continue to show up for yourself, your breathing eventually slows, and you begin to inhabit your own life.

The Olive Man had stories that filled the air. He had a lifetime of adventures to draw on for stories. I stayed quiet. My past felt too heavy to share. It took more than twenty-five years before he heard all of it. I had learned that people could weaponize your history, and honesty felt risky.

We kept separate bank accounts at my insistence. I was terrified of being left penniless again. Even though I trusted him, I needed proof that I could stand on my own while standing beside someone else.

Leaving a bad situation isn't enough. You have to build something new, often without a blueprint. I wanted healthy love and clear boundaries. I knew I was healing the day I told him I would no longer wash his oatmeal pan—the one he always left by the sink to dry into a sticky cement. I had washed it countless times, resentment quietly growing with each scrub. Instead of letting that resentment spoil the marriage, I learned to say no. Simple in theory. Monumental in practice. When people react angrily to your boundaries, they reveal how entitled they have been. The Olive Man laughed and said he never expected me to wash it anyway. That was when I laughed too. My church-lady training had convinced me that Jesus Christ himself might appear and judge a dried oatmeal pan on the counter. In truth, I doubted I was important enough for such a visit, and if he did arrive, there were far more important things to discuss.

It wasn't just a bad first marriage that shaped me. It was family, church, and society that taught the wrong lessons. It was also living through moments that happened to me without the ability to create meaning for them—meaning that came from my own true north, not one handed to me by others. Counseling and countless self-help books helped me find my true north and understand what healthy love actually looked like.

Over time, I saw patterns passed through generations of women— my mother, my grandmother. I learned how to interrupt them and build new ones. The Olive Man's kindness stopped feeling like danger. His care stopped feeling like a trap. Our marriage was strengthened in a quiet counselor's office, with a box of tissues on the side table and hard questions asked.

I learned healthy love doesn't depend on silence for safety; it holds room for you to speak your truth. We started healing together as a couple, and I began my lifelong personal healing journey.

Our life doesn't have a perfect ending; we are not chasing perfection. There are still hard days and old ghosts. But now we have tools and understanding. For the first time, I wasn't surviving alone. I was in a partnership.

Time doesn't heal wounds by itself. Healing takes work, honesty, courage, and learning how to love and be loved. At times, it felt like we were trying to grow a garden on my scorched earth, and he would look for every reason not to be home. But between the conversations, the quiet mornings, and the brave apologies, something real took root.

We laugh more now. Old wounds surface, but they don't cut as deeply. Counseling changed everything. Writing this story changed everything, too. Seeing my life clearly laid out on paper helped me understand patterns and avoid repeating them.

I never knew how valuable it would be to wake up without fear—to put the knife back in the kitchen drawer instead of under my pillow. Letting love land without suspicion remains part of my recovery.

When my stepdaughter once said, "I believe in you," the words stunned me. No one had ever said that before. To be believed in is soul changing.

Love did not arrive as a rescue or a reward. It came quietly, in shared meals, ordinary conversations, and days that did not require bracing. After the storm of my life, love became something warm and steady—a place that finally felt like home.

I learned that I was not too late, not too broken, and not too far gone to grow a life of my own.

"The most common way people give up their power is by thinking they don't have any."

~ Alice Walker

Almost Final Words

With my life story I just shared, you should know I spoke to you *"from the scar, not the wound"* —a great quote by Glennon Doyle. My healing will be lifelong, but I now participate in it joyfully, and in a house that finally reflects the woman I've become, not the girl I had to be to survive.

For most of my life, I lived in houses built out of fear, silence, and smallness. They were battlegrounds and prisons, places where I learned to endure rather than to live. Each house held a chapter of my becoming, shaping me in ways I didn't understand then.

Houses are more than places to store your belongings. They hold memories, secrets, and struggles. Every home I lived in became another chapter of my life, some filled with hunger, fear, or the simple stubborn need to survive. I used to believe that if I just found the right house, with the right person, everything would finally hold together.

But the truth is this: safety was never inside the house.

I had to find it in myself.

The hardest part of leaving isn't walking out the door. It's convincing yourself that you're allowed to walk, that you are worthy of the journey. Even after I escaped, I carried pieces of those old houses inside me. The shame. The fear. The doubt. They don't disappear overnight

Healing is not a straight road. It's a mess it is messy, painful, and full of moments when you wonder if you've made yet another mistake. But here is what I've learned:

That better life?

It's worth fighting for.

No house, no person, and no past mistake gets to define you. You can reclaim your life. You can break free. And if no one else has told you this yet, let me be the one: ***You deserve better.***

Things I Wish I Had Known

- **Know yourself first.** Understand who you are and who you want to be before tying yourself to someone else. Set your boundaries early, and know your worth.

- **Gaslighting is real.** If you feel like you're constantly questioning your own reality, trust your instincts.

- **Abusers don't always "look" like abusers.** They can be charming, admired, even loved by others—not for how they treat you, but for the image they project. Often, they do for others what they refuse to do for you, because it makes them look good.

- **Leaving is a process, not a single event.** It takes planning, courage, and sometimes multiple attempts. That doesn't mean you failed—it means you are still fighting for your freedom.

- **Your life after abuse is worth fighting for.** The path won't be easy, but you will be free. And freedom is the beginning of everything.

- **Abuse is never your fault.** Nothing you said or did makes you deserve mistreatment.

- **Control is not love.** Real love doesn't require you to shrink, submit, or silence yourself to keep the peace.

- **Isolation is a tactic.** If someone tries to cut you off from friends, family, or community, that is abuse, not protection.

- **Apologies without change are manipulation.** Words mean little without actions that match.

- **Your voice matters.** Speaking your truth—whether whispered to a friend or written in a journal—is an act of reclaiming power.

- **Healing takes time.** Some days you'll feel strong, other days broken. Both are normal, and neither means you're failing.

- **Help is out there.** Even if you feel invisible, there are hotlines, shelters, and people ready to listen and believe you.

A Warning From the Past

When I left my marriage, I thought I was escaping a time and place where women had few rights, where the law and the culture around me made it nearly impossible to break free. I struggled my way out, found my voice, and reclaimed my life. But as I watch the world around me now, I see the shadows of that past rising again.

New laws and policies are being introduced that could make it harder for women to leave unhealthy, abusive, or simply unhappy marriages. Some states are attempting to roll back no-fault divorce, meaning women could once again have to prove abuse, adultery, or abandonment just to escape.[1] Others are pushing for "covenant marriages" that would severely restrict grounds for divorce and make separation nearly impossible.[2] In Texas, for example, proposed legislation aims to limit no-fault divorce even further, trapping individuals in marriages that should never have had to continue.[3]

Even financial independence is being challenged. Some proposals would make it harder for women to access their own financial resources or reclaim their names after marriage.[4]

The consequences of such laws are not speculative; they are well-documented. Research shows that when no-fault divorce became widely available, rates of domestic violence, suicide among women, and even spousal homicide declined.[5] Scholars such as Dobash and Dobash have long shown how social and legal structures shape women's vulnerability and ability to escape abuse.[6] Restricting access to divorce will not save marriages; it will condemn many to suffering.

Since I first wrote these words, the threats to freedom have grown even more real. Bills like the SAVE Act now seek to require proof of citizenship just to register to vote, adding new barriers for eligible citizens.[7][8] At the same time, states are introducing laws that would limit or roll back a woman's access to contraception, restrict reproductive health providers, and impose harsher clinical regulations.[9] Divorce laws remain under pressure, with proposals in Texas, Oklahoma, and South Carolina that push for more fault-based requirements or spousal-consent rules, making it more challenging than ever to leave unwanted marriages.[10]

None of this is hypothetical. It is unfolding in real time.

When I left, I didn't have a good safety net. I had to struggle for every bit of freedom I won. And yet, I had more legal options than many women may have in the future, if these laws take hold. I write my story not only to share my past, but to sound a warning. If you are in a marriage that feels suffocating and you sense that your freedom is slipping away, know that you are not imagining it. The world is shifting in ways that could make leaving even harder. Do not wait until the door locks behind you.

Learn your rights. Pay attention to the laws in your state. If you're thinking about leaving, start planning now. No one should have to live without freedom.

To those who have never lived this kind of life, who believe that these laws are about preserving marriage or family values, I urge you to listen to the voices of those of us who have been there. Stripping women of their ability to leave is not about preserving families. It is about control.[11]

Already, these threats are more than theory. They have already caused deaths.

According to reporting by ProPublica, Josseli Barnica died in Texas after doctors delayed emergency miscarriage care, fearing they would violate abortion laws.[12] As *The Guardian* documented, another

Texas woman, Porsha Ngumezi, bled to death when doctors avoided a standard procedure for miscarriage care for the same reason.[13] In Georgia, news reports confirm that Amber Nicole Thurman's death from septic shock was linked to a preventable delay in treatment caused by abortion restrictions.[14]

My heart and soul feel broken for these families, for the loss of lives that could have been prevented.

These are not "what-ifs" or warnings from the distant past. *They are tragedies happening now, the human cost of laws that put ideology above survival.*

As I write these words, I am watching the walls of that old prison being rebuilt for another generation of women. If we do not speak out and fight back, we will wake up in a world where leaving is no longer an option. And I cannot, in good conscience, stay silent.

History is repeating itself. We cannot allow it to close the doors we've fought so hard to open.

Note to Readers: This section draws on my own lived experience, along with public reporting and legal sources available at the time of writing. It is not meant as a prediction, a legal judgment, or an accusation, but as a reflection on how patterns from the past can echo forward. Readers are invited to consider these warnings thoughtfully and in context, not as a final authority.

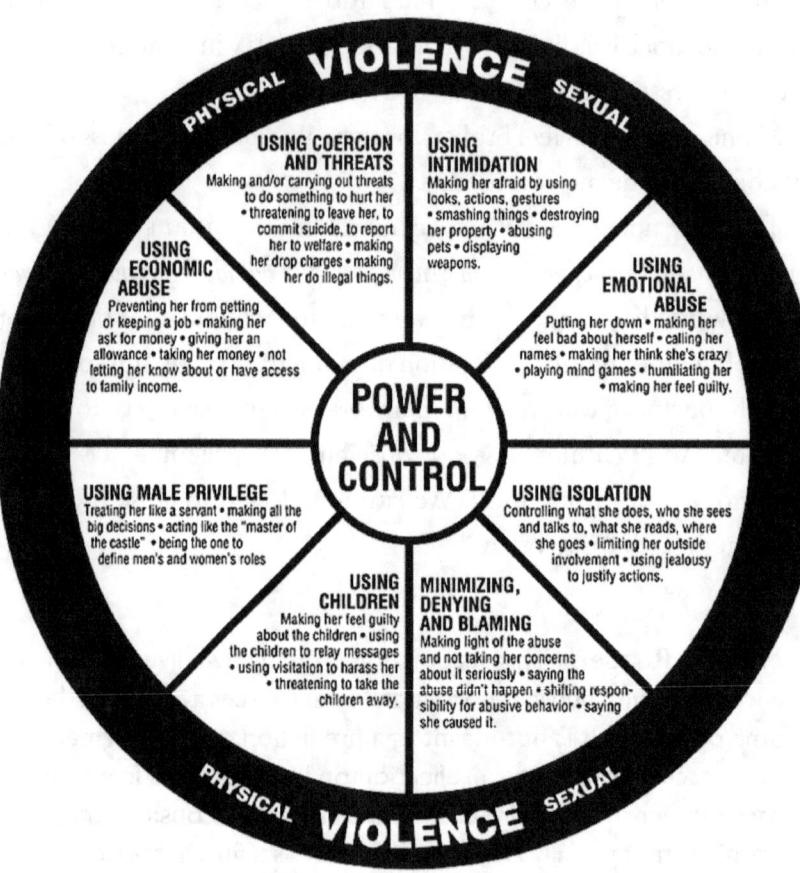

Credit: Domestic Abuse Intervention Programs
202 East Superior Street   Duluth, MN 55802   218-722-2781
www.theduluthmodel.org

The Cycle of Violence

The cycle of violence describes a repeating pattern of abuse that escalates over time. Understanding these phases helps reveal how control and harm are maintained in abusive relationships.

1. Tension Building

- Stress and conflict increase.
- The abuser may become irritable, controlling, quiet, or emotionally distant.
- Victims often feel they must 'walk on eggshells' and try to appease the abuser to prevent an outburst.

2. Incident

- The abuser lashes out through physical, verbal, emotional, or psychological abuse.
- This may include threats, insults, intimidation, coercion (forcing someone through threats or pressure), or physical violence.
- Victims experience fear, pain, and helplessness.

3. Reconciliation (the 'Honeymoon Phase')

- The abuser apologizes, makes excuses, or minimizes the harm.
- They may blame external factors or promise to change.
- Some show affection through gifts or by acting as though nothing happened.
- Victims may hope the abuse has ended and believe the promises.

4. Calm (Period of Normalcy)

- The relationship appears stable, and the abuser may act as though they have changed.

- Life feels peaceful, but the underlying issues remain unresolved.

- Over time, tension gradually returns, restarting the cycle.

Recognizing and understanding this cycle is crucial for identifying patterns of abuse and finding ways to break free.

Resources

1. Domestic Violence & Crisis Support

- **National Domestic Violence Hotline (U.S.)** — 1-800-799-SAFE (7233) or thehotline.org for 24/7 confidential support.

- **National Coalition Against Domestic Violence (NCADV)** — ncadv.org

- **State & Local Resources** — Readers are encouraged to look up their state's DV shelters, legal aid, and crisis services.

2. Safety Planning & Legal Help

- **Domestic Shelters Website** — domesticshelters.org, searchable by ZIP code.

- **RAINN (Rape, Abuse & Incest National Network)** — 1-800-656-HOPE (4673) or rainn.org

- WomensLaw.org — Legal protections including restraining orders, custody, and divorce information.

3. Financial & Independence Resources

- **Purple Purse** — hollyshouse.org, helping survivors regain financial independence.

- **CareerOneStop** — careeronestop.org, job training and career rebuilding.

4. Mental Health & Healing

- **Crisis Text Line** — Text HOME to 741741 for free 24/7 crisis counseling.

- **BetterHelp** — betterhelp.com online therapy, useful for those who are isolated.

- **SAMHSA (Substance Abuse and Mental Health Services Administration)** — 1-800-662-HELP (4357) or samhsa.gov

- **The Trevor Project (LGBTQ+ Support)** — 1-866-488-7386 or text START to 678678 or thetrevorproject.org

- **The Mighty** — themighty.com online mental health support community.

- ***The Body Keeps the Score*** by Bessel van der Kolk book on healing www.besselvanderkolk.com/resources/the-body-keeps-the-score

5. International Support

- **Canada** — sheltersafe.ca Talk Suicide Canada: 1-833-456-4566

- **United Kingdom** — Women's Aid, womensaid.org.uk/ 0808 2000 247 (24/7 Domestic Abuse Helpline)

- **Australia** — 1800respect.org.au 1-800-RESPECT (1-800-737-7328)

- **Global** — rainn.org - RAINN's International Support List, a directory of organizations worldwide.

Citations and Penal Codes

The penal codes listed here in the resource section are not charges that were ever filed. They represent possible applications under California law and are included to illustrate the legal implications of the situations I describe. They are meant as context only, not as records of any persecution.

CHAPTER ONE — The First Click
LEGAL CITATIONS AND END NOTES

1. **Cults:** Many experts define *cults* as high-control groups led by authoritarian figures who use psychological manipulation and strict rules to limit members' freedom and isolate them from outsiders (Hassan 1990; Singer 1995; American Psychological Association, "Cults and New Religious Movements"). Such groups often discourage independent thought and maintain obedience through fear and social pressure.

   American Psychological Association. *APA Dictionary of Psychology*, s.v. "Cults and New Religious Movements." Defines cults as "groups characterized by highly structured belief systems, charismatic leadership, and intense social control."

   Steven Hassan. *Combating Cult Mind Control.* Rochester, VT: Park Street Press, 1990. Explains how cults manipulate and control members through psychological influence and obedience conditioning.

   Margaret Thaler Singer. *Cults in Our Midst: The Hidden Menace in Our Everyday Lives.* San Francisco: Jossey-Bass, 1995. Identifies common characteristics and mind-control techniques used by destructive groups.

   The Church I grew up in: *"Like many high-control religious groups, the church I grew up in had strict rules, enforced obedience, and used fear to keep members in line. Some experts classify such groups as cults because of their authoritarian structure and manipulation tactics (Hassan, 1990; Singer, 1995; and the American Psychological Association. "Cults and New Religious Movements."*

   The Worldwide Church of God (WCG) underwent significant transformations from its peak in the 1970s and 1980s, to its reformation in the 1990s.

   Origins and Teachings in the 1970s and 1980s:
   • Herbert W. Armstrong founded the WCG in the 1930s, and it was initially known as the Radio Church of God. Armstrong's teachings

combined elements from various religious doctrines, leading to a unique set of beliefs often termed "Armstrongism." Key characteristics during this period included:

- British Israelism: The belief that the British and American peoples were descendants of the ten lost tribes of Israel.

- Non-Trinitarian Theology: A rejection of the traditional Christian doctrine of the Trinity.

- Observance of Old Testament Laws: Strict adherence to seventh-day Sabbath observance, dietary restrictions, clothing restrictions, and makeup and wig bans for women.

- Authoritarian Leadership: Armstrong maintained centralized control over church doctrines and practices.

- The WCG was often labeled a cult during this era because of its unorthodox beliefs and practices.

2. **"Jonestown Massacre." Encyclopedia Britannica.** Accessed August 31, 2025. https://www.britannica.com/event/Jonestown. My church often practiced what's called *eisegesis*: forcing its own meaning into the Bible. ***Eisegesis:*** *Reading your own ideas into the Bible instead of drawing meaning out of the text itself.*

CHAPTER THREE — The Night Before
LEGAL CITATIONS AND END NOTES

1. **California Penal Code § 647.6:** Child Molestation
This statute makes it a crime to annoy or molest any child under 18 years of age. While often applied to less severe conduct, it can encompass a range of inappropriate behaviors. *California Penal Code § 243.4* defines sexual battery as the non-consensual touching of an intimate part of another person, clothed or unclothed, for sexual purposes. Because minors cannot legally consent, such contact with a child under 18 is classified as sexual assault.

CHAPTER FOUR — Broken Dreams
LEGAL CITATIONS AND END NOTES

1. **California Labor Code § 230** and related laws protect a person's right to work without interference.
2. **California Penal Code § 594:** Vandalism/malicious mischief – could apply to throwing away belongings such as college books.

3. **California Penal Code § 13700 and California Family Code § 6320(c):** define abuse to include isolating, intimidating, or controlling a spouse, and destroying their property. What was previously invisible would now be recognized as a form of abuse under the law.

4. The Greek word *kephalē* (κεφαλή), often translated "head," literally means the physical head but can also mean "source" or "origin," as in the headwaters of a river. In classical and Hellenistic Greek, it was rarely used to mean "leader" or "authority." Some modern scholars argue that passages such as *Ephesians 5:23* and *1 Corinthians 11:3* are better understood as describing man as the "source" of woman (as in Genesis 2), rather than granting husbands authority over wives. See Catherine C. Kroeger and Richard Clark Kroeger, *I Suffer Not a Woman* (Grand Rapids: Baker, 1992), 141–160; Gordon D. Fee, *Listening to the Spirit in the Text* (Grand Rapids: Eerdmans, 2000), 55–57.

CHAPTER FIVE — House of Non-Consent
LEGAL CITATIONS AND END NOTES

Before 1979, many states, including California, had laws that exempted spouses from being prosecuted for rape based on outdated notions of marital consent being irrevocable.

In 1979, California's legislature passed a law recognizing that rape can occur within a marriage, holding spouses accountable for sexual assault.

California's change in 1979 was a significant step forward in recognizing marital rape as a crime and addressing issues of domestic violence and sexual assault. Other states followed over the years, but it wasn't until 1993 that marital rape was illegal in all 50 U.S. states.

Diana E. H. Russell, *Rape in Marriage* (Bloomington: Indiana University Press, 1990); see also Jill Filipovic, "How Marital Rape Became a Crime in the US," *The Guardian*, Aug. 7, 2019. The last two states to criminalize marital rape were North Carolina and Oklahoma in 1993.

1. **California Penal Code § 236:** False imprisonment for restricting movement and freedom without consent.

2. **California Family Code § 721:** Breach of fiduciary duty to act fairly and respectfully within marriage.

3. **California Penal Code § 646.9:** Stalking and creating emotional distress through coercion and monitoring.

4. **California Evidence Code § 1101(b):** Patterns of abusive behavior and psychological manipulation.
5. **California Penal Code § 243(e)(1):** Domestic battery involving willful and unlawful force.
6. **California Penal Code § 422:** Criminal threats for verbal intimidation and physical domination.
7. **California Penal Code § 261(a):** Rape, as defined by sexual intercourse without consent.
8. **California Penal Code § 261.6:** Lack of affirmative consent during sexual activity.
9. **California Penal Code § 243(e)(1):** Domestic battery through physical and emotional harm.
10. **California Penal Code § 273.5(a):** Infliction of corporal injury on a spouse resulting in traumatic conditions.
11. **California Penal Code § 422:** Criminal threats for verbal intimidation and physical domination.
12. **California Family Code § 752:** Equal mutual consent in marital sexual relations.
13. **California Penal Code § 12022.7:** Injury resulting in bodily harm during a felony act.
14. **California Evidence Code § 1160:** Patterns of psychological trauma inflicted by abuse.
15. **California Evidence Code § 1101(b):** Patterns of coercive control and abuse.
16. **California Health and Safety Code § 124174.3:** Maternal emotional health and its impacts on fetal development.

CHAPTER SIX — The Church That Raised Me
LEGAL CITATIONS AND END NOTES

1. The American Academy of Pediatrics does not recommend routine circumcision for all male infants, though it notes modest health benefits such as reduced risk of urinary tract infections, penile cancer, and certain sexually transmitted infections. Most males will never require circumcision for medical reasons, though the procedure may be advised later in life for conditions such as recurrent infections or phimosis. See American Academy of Pediatrics Task Force on Circumcision, "Circumcision Policy Statement," *Pediatrics* 130, no. 3 (September 2012): 585–586.

2. "The Worldwide Church of God claimed over 140,000 members at its peak." Remnant of The Worldwide Church of God. The Church and its members were thriving... Accessed 2025.

3. "The church was featured on *60 Minutes* in 1979, where Mike Wallace interviewed critics and former members." Segment summary: Worldwide Church of God, CBS *60 Minutes*, 1979.

4. "By the late 1990s, over 80% of WCG's membership left the organization due to doctrinal changes." *Christianity Today*, ibid.

5. Splinter groups such as the United Church of God and Living Church of God emerged from disillusioned WCG members following schisms. See Wikipedia, "Worldwide Church of God," and David Francis, Religion Watch, "Worldwide Church of God dissolves, leaving replica splinter groups in its wake" Accessed 8/31/2025.

6. "In the 1990s, the church was renamed Grace Communion International, renouncing previous doctrines and aligning with mainstream evangelical Christianity." Grace Communion International, "History of Our Church."

CHAPTER SEVEN — House of No Money
LEGAL CITATIONS AND END NOTES

In today's market of 2024, if a man had to pay for all the things a wife quietly does—cooking, cleaning, caring, managing—he'd be writing checks that could rival a professional's salary. In today's market, homemaker services can cost nearly $70,000 a year, and yet across the globe, women's unpaid care adds up to an almost unthinkable $11 trillion annually.

Oxfam, "Not All Gaps Are Created Equal: The True Value of Care Work." 2020. Estimated that the global economic value of unpaid care work is nearly $11 trillion annually. https://www.oxfam.org/en/not-all-gaps-are-created-equal-true-value-care-work

Nurse Next Door, "How Much Does Senior Home Care Cost?" 2023. Lists homemaker services at an average of ~$68,640 annually, and home health aide services at ~$75,504 annually. https://www.nursenextdoor.com/blog/how-much-does-senior-home-care-cost

1. Cap Radio. "Segregated Sacramento: A History of Housing Discrimination." 2017. https://www.capradio.org/news/the-view-from-here/2017/08/15/s10-e2-transcript-segregated-sacramento

2. Southern Poverty Law Center. "Racist Skinhead David Lynch Reemerges as Leader of Sacramento's American Front." https://www.splcenter.org/resources/reports/racist-skinhead-david-lynch-reemerges-leader-sacramentos-american-front

3. **Financial Abuse:** The restriction of access to money, the requirement to ask for necessities, and controlling all financial decisions meet the definition of coercive control under many modern domestic violence laws.

4. **Theft California Penal Code 484(a):** Unauthorized taking of money, especially funds intended for a child's needs, can be classified as petty theft.

   California Penal Code § 368: Neglect of a dependent spouse or children by withholding resources such as money for diapers, pads, or shoes constitutes a form of abuse.

5. **Economic Abuse and Coercion:** Many states now recognize economic coercion as part of domestic abuse laws, emphasizing how financial control can entrap victims in abusive relationships.

CHAPTER EIGHT — House of Hunger
LEGAL CITATIONS AND END NOTES

1. **Neglect and Deprivation California Penal Code § 368** (Elder and Dependent Adult Abuse): While this typically applies to elder or dependent adults, withholding food and necessary resources from dependents (e.g., a pregnant spouse and young children) may constitute neglect or abuse.

   California Penal Code § 270: Willful neglect or failure to provide necessities for a minor child (e.g., food, shelter, or medical care) is a criminal offense. A parent's responsibility includes ensuring their children have adequate food.

2. **Child Endangerment California Penal Code § 273a:** Causing or permitting a child to suffer unjustifiable physical pain or mental suffering, or placing a child in a situation where their health is endangered. Exposing children to prolonged hunger or unsafe environments may qualify under this statute.

3. **Emotional and Psychological Abuse California Family Code § 6320:** Emotional abuse, including deprivation of necessities, threats, and

creating an environment of fear, falls under the definition of domestic violence in California.

4. **Margarette "Mama" Marks** was a cherished community volunteer and philanthropist in North Sacramento, particularly in the Del Paso Heights area. In 1972, she founded the Arms of March Program, which provided meals to residents in need. Her dedication to alleviating hunger and supporting her community spanned the 1970s through the early 1990s. In recognition of her significant contributions, a local park was named in her honor in 2000. Today, Margarette "Mama" Marks Park stands as a testament to her enduring legacy and the positive impact she had on the Del Paso Heights community.

5. **Financial Abuse and Coercive Control California Family Code § 6320:** Coercive control includes isolating a person from financial resources or necessities. Restricting access to money, food, and transportation (e.g., preventing the renewal of your driver's license) reflects financial abuse and coercive control.

6. **Threats and Intimidation California Penal Code § 422:** Criminal threats involve statements or actions intended to create fear of harm. Threatening you over food provided by your mother and creating a hostile environment are examples of intimidation.

7. **False Imprisonment California Penal Code § 236:** Preventing you from leaving the house or seeking help (e.g., riding a bike to a food bank) constitutes false imprisonment.

8. **Exploitation of Dependence California Penal Code § 368(b) (1):** If an individual knowingly exploits the dependence of a spouse or children for control, it may fall under abuse laws.

9. **Domestic Violence - California Penal Code § 13700:** Domestic violence includes abuse against a spouse, including physical, emotional, and psychological harm. Denying food and resources contributes to an abusive environment.

10. **Alcohol-Fueled Endangerment California Penal Code § 647(f):** Public intoxication leading to harm or danger applies more broadly, but alcohol-fueled abuse and neglect within the home contribute to endangerment and abuse.

CHAPTER NINE — House of Choking
LEGAL CITATIONS AND END NOTES

1. **Medical Neglect California Health and Safety Code § 11162.5:** Neglecting necessary medical treatments or interfering with medical care, as seen in the rough handling of the eye medication for your baby, could be considered medical neglect or endangerment.

2. **Physical Abuse: Assault and Battery – California Penal Code § 240 (Assault):** The act of choking and backhanding you constitutes assault, as it involved an unlawful attempt to inflict violent injury.
   California Penal Code § 242 (Battery): Physical contact that causes harm or offensive contact, such as choking and hitting, qualifies as battery.

3. **Domestic Violence – California Penal Code § 273.5:** Infliction of corporal injury resulting in a traumatic condition. The bruises around your neck would constitute evidence of a traumatic condition under this law.
   California Penal Code § 13700: Domestic violence encompasses abuse against a current or former spouse or cohabitant, including physical and emotional harm.

4. **Child Endangerment – California Penal Code § 273a:** Causing or permitting a child to suffer unjustifiable physical pain or mental suffering. By refusing to provide food, controlling access to necessities, and exposing the children to an abusive environment, this statute may apply.

5. **Coercive Control – California Family Code § 6320:** Coercive control includes isolating someone from resources, financial control, and deprivation of basic needs. Preventing you from driving, accessing money, or leaving to find food fits this description.

6. **Gaslighting:** Gaslighting is a form of psychological manipulation where an individual seeks to make another person doubt their own perceptions, memories, or sanity. This tactic often involves denying facts, trivializing the victim's feelings, or presenting false information, leading the victim to question their reality and become increasingly dependent on the perpetrator.

7. **False Imprisonment – California Penal Code § 236:** Unlawfully restraining or confining someone's freedom of movement. Preventing you from leaving the house or obtaining essential resources, such as food, constitutes false imprisonment.

8. **Planned Parenthood** is a nonprofit organization that provides high-quality, affordable sexual and reproductive health care for all people, as well as being the nation's largest provider of sex education.

9. **Threats and Emotional Abuse – California Penal Code § 422:** Criminal threats include any statement or action that intentionally creates fear of harm. Telling you he would prevent you from seeing your children and ensuring you were viewed as a bad mother could qualify as a form of emotional abuse and threats.

CHAPTER TEN — The House of Turning Wheels
LEGAL CITATIONS AND END NOTES

1. **Economic Abuse & Coercive Control (Domestic Violence Laws)** – Restricting access to money, preventing work, and financial coercion fall under domestic abuse statutes in many states.

2. **Coercion to Quit Employment** – Laws addressing economic coercion recognize that forcing a spouse to quit work is a form of financial control.

3. **Inheritance Coercion (Financial Abuse)** – Forcing a spouse to surrender or misuse an inheritance can violate marital property laws and financial abuse protections.

4. **Vehicle Vandalism (California Penal Code § 594):** Willfully deflating another person's tires, damaging a vehicle, or preventing its use can be charged as criminal vandalism if the cost to repair exceeds a certain threshold.

5. **Restricting Access to Transportation (Coercive Control Laws)** – Restricting a partner's ability to drive, obtain a license, or maintain independent mobility is recognized as a form of domestic abuse under various state laws.

6. **Child Endangerment (California Penal Code § 273a):** Leaving children in the care of an intoxicated parent or exposing them to dangerous situations can constitute child endangerment.

7. **Child Neglect (Child Welfare Statutes)** – Failing to protect a child from known harm can be considered neglect, even if the caregiver believes they are making the best choice.

8. **Financial Abuse (Domestic Violence Laws)** – Using household finances for addiction while neglecting family needs constitutes financial abuse.

9. The ILO estimates the value of unpaid care and domestic work to be as much as 9 percent of global GDP (USD 11 trillion). APEC+2World Economic Forum+2

   At the global level, valued at an hourly minimum wage, this unpaid care work would constitute 9 % of global GDP, amounting to USD 11 trillion. UNDP+1

   The national hourly cost for homemaker services, Hourly $33. CareScout

CHAPTER ELEVEN — House of Changing Wind
LEGAL CITATIONS AND END NOTES

1. **The cycle of violence** is a repeating pattern in abusive relationships where tension builds, violence erupts, and is followed by a "honeymoon" phase of apologies or calm before the cycle begins again. (See the resources page in this book for more, or your city's DVC office.)

2. **False Imprisonment – California Penal Code § 236:** Unlawfully restraining or confining someone's freedom of movement. Preventing you from leaving the house or obtaining essential resources, such as food, constitutes false imprisonment.

   California Penal Code § 236: false imprisonment is defined as: *"The unlawful violation of the personal liberty of another."*

   Key Elements of False Imprisonment:
   To prove false imprisonment, the following elements must generally be present:
   a. **Intentional Restraint** – The perpetrator intentionally confined or restricted the victim's movement.
   b. **Without Consent** – The victim did not agree to be confined.
   c. **No Legal Authority** – The act was not legally justified.
   d. **Any Means of Confinement** – Physical barriers (such as a locked gate), force, threats, or deceit used to restrict a person's movement.

CHAPTER TWELVE — Freedom
LEGAL CITATIONS AND END NOTES

1. **California Penal Code § 422: Criminal Threats** – This law makes it a crime to threaten to kill or seriously harm someone if:
   - The threat is made verbally, in writing, or electronically.
   - The person being threatened reasonably fears for their safety.
   - The threat is specific and unconditional.
   - The person making the threat has the apparent ability to carry it out.

In this case, his admission that he would have killed you had he found you could be seen as a criminal threat, especially given the history of abuse and control. If this statement caused fear or was taken seriously at the time, it could have been a prosecutable offense.

2. **Failure to Pay Child Support (California Family Code 4700)** – A parent's failure to contribute financially to the well-being of **their** children can result in legal consequences.

3. **Coercive Control (Financial Abuse Laws)** – Controlling a spouse's earnings, withholding funds, or limiting financial independence can be prosecuted under financial abuse statutes.

CHAPTER THIRTEEN — House of Shack
LEGAL CITATIONS AND END NOTES

1. **Personal Responsibility and Work Opportunity Reconciliation Act of 1996, Pub. L. No. 104-193, 110 Stat. 2105 (1996).** This legislation transformed the Aid to Families with Dependent Children (AFDC) program into the Temporary Assistance for Needy Families (TANF) program, changing welfare policies nationwide.

2. **California Department of Social Services, CalWORKs Program Overview**, available at **https://www.cdss.ca.gov/calworks**. CalWORKs serves as California's implementation of TANF, requiring participants to engage in work-related activities to receive benefits.

3. In 1997, the federal government spent only 9.9% of its budget on all welfare-related programs combined—and it wasn't just cash assistance for single moms. This funding covered a wide range of vital services for millions of struggling Americans, including:

   ◆ Medicaid (6.6%) – Providing healthcare for low-income families, children, pregnant women, and the disabled.

   ◆ Supplemental Security Income (SSI) – Supporting elderly, blind, and disabled individuals who can't work.

   ◆ Food Stamps (SNAP) & Housing Aid – Helping low-income working families, veterans, and the disabled afford food and shelter.

   ◆ Temporary Assistance for Needy Families (TANF) – The smallest portion, offering limited cash aid to low-income parents with strict work requirements.

4. In 1990, U.S. defense spending totaled approximately $299 billion and declined slightly during the decade, reaching around $294.5 billion by 2000 https://www.econlib.org/archives/2012/08/us_federal_budg.html. That sum equates to roughly $90 per person per month when apportioned evenly across an estimated U.S. population of about 260–280 million at the time.

5. The 1996 welfare reform law (PRWORA) replaced AFDC with TANF, instituting limited-duration benefits and mandatory work requirements, even for those earning low wages, as part of a broader national emphasis on reducing dependence on public assistance across the 1990s https://sgp.fas.org/crs/misc/R43400.pdf?

   In the 1990s, despite no major recession, welfare reform became a political priority. Leaders promised to reduce dependence on government aid, and programs like TANF (Temporary Assistance for Needy Families), which required recipients to enter the workforce, even if those jobs paid unlivable wages.

6. The term "welfare queen" became infamous in the 1980s through political rhetoric portraying women as abusing the system for personal gain. This stereotype, largely based on misrepresentations and isolated cases, persisted in public discourse despite evidence that most welfare recipients used aid temporarily and for essential survival needs. See NPR, *"The Truth Behind the Lies of the Original Welfare Queen,"* December 20, 2013. The Personal Responsibility and Work Opportunity Reconciliation Act of 1996, Pub. L. No. 104-193, 110 Stat. 2105 (1996), replaced AFDC with TANF and reshaped welfare policies nationwide.

   The biggest recipients of "welfare" weren't single mothers; they were disabled individuals, elderly retirees, and working families who couldn't make ends meet. But politicians used false stereotypes like the "welfare queen" to demonize the poor while ignoring the billions in corporate subsidies and tax breaks handed to the wealthy.

   The truth? Welfare wasn't bankrupting America. It was helping people survive.

7. Tom T. Hall, *Harper Valley P.T.A.*, performed by Jeannie C. Riley. Plantation Records, 1968, vinyl.

CHAPTER FIFTEEN — House of After
LEGAL CITATIONS AND END NOTES

1. van der Kolk, B. (2014). *The Body Keeps the Score: Brain, Mind, and Body in theHealing of Trauma*. Viking.
2. Bremner, J. D. (2006). "Traumatic stress: effects on the brain." Dialogues in Clinical Neuroscience, 8(4), 445–461. [PMCID: PMC3181836]

A WARNING FROM THE PAST
LEGAL CITATIONS AND END NOTES

1. Roth, M. *No-Fault Divorce Under Threat: The Battle Over Marital Freedom. Family Law Review* 45, no. 3 (2023): 217–235.

2. Smith, J. *Covenant Marriage Laws and Their Impact on Divorce Rates. Journal of Legal Studies* 39, no. 2 (2022): 88–101.

3. Texas House Bill 3188 (2024) proposed changes to no-fault divorce statutes in Texas.

4. National Women's Law Center. *Financial Independence and Marital Law: Proposed Restrictions in 2024.*

5. Stevenson, B., and Wolfers, J. "Bargaining in the Shadow of the Law: Divorce Laws and Family Distress." *Quarterly Journal of Economics* 121, no. 1 (2006): 267–288.

6. Dobash, R. E., and Dobash, R. P. *Women, Violence and Social Change.* Routledge, 1992.

7. H.R.22 — *SAVE Act (Safeguard American Voter Eligibility Act)*, 119th Congress (2025). Congress.gov.

8. Voting Rights Lab. "2025 Legislative Sessions to Date: Key Election Policy Trends." VotingRightsLab.org.

9. National Women's Law Center. "The Trump Administration's First Actions in 2025 Targeting Patients, Providers, and Reproductive Health Care Access." NWLC.org.

10. Washington State Bar Association Blog. "The History and Future of No-Fault Divorce in the U.S., December 2024. nwsidebar.wsba.org.

11. National Women's Law Center. Financial Independence and Marital Law: Proposed Restrictions in 2024.

12. ProPublica. "She Died After a Delayed Miscarriage. The Doctor Said It Would Have Been a Crime to Treat Her Sooner." July 2024. propublica.org.

13. The Guardian. "Texas Woman Dies After Miscarriage Complications Amid Abortion Ban." November 25, 2024. theguardian.com.

14. "Death of Amber Thurman." Wikipedia. Accessed September 2025. en.wikipedia.org.

About the Author

Boni Woodland is an artist, writer, and survivor with a deep love for storytelling that heals, inspires, and empowers. Her memoir, *Turning Survival Into Words—From Houses of Fear to Freedom*, shares her journey of resilience, escape, and finding freedom after years of hardship. Through her writing, she hopes to shed light on the realities of domestic abuse while offering hope to those seeking their own path to safety and self-discovery.

When she's not writing, Boni paints and creates connections through her art. She believes in the power of nature, kindness, and the strength that can be found in every person's story.

Follow her journey in her art, memoir, and future stories at **penandbrushink.blogspot.com** and **www.painterandthreads.com**.